THE SECRETS OF SPIRITUAL POWER

THE JOY OF BELIEVING PRAYER

JOYCE MEYER

WARNER *Faith*

New York • Boston • Nashville

THE SECRETS OF
SPIRITUAL POWER

CONTENTS

CONTENTS

THE JOY OF
ＢELIEVING PRAYER

CONTENTS

THE SECRETS OF
SPIRITUAL POWER

BEHOLD YOUR GOD

God is always working in secret, behind the scenes, even when it feels as though nothing will ever change. For change to be lasting, it must come from the inside out. Only God can effect that type of heart change. Let God be God!

GOD'S WORD FOR YOU

What then shall we say to [all] this? If God is for us, who [can be] against us? [Who can be our foe, if God is on our side?]

ROMANS 8:31

Those who trust in, lean on, and confidently hope in the Lord are like Mount Zion, which cannot be moved but abides and stands fast forever.

As the mountains are round about Jerusalem, so the Lord is round about His people from this time forth and forever.

PSALM 125:1–2

one

BEHOLD YOUR GOD

God is a big God; nothing is impossible with Him. We have nothing to fear from our enemies because none of them are as great as our God.

God is for us; He is on our side. The devil has one position—he is against us. But God is over us, under us, through us, for us, and He surrounds us. Of whom, then, should we be afraid?

So like Mount Zion, we should never be moved because God is all around us. And if that wasn't enough, I saved the best until last: He is in us, and He said that He will never leave us or forsake us.

Salvation is our most awesome blessing from God, and we have been given the Helper, the Holy Spirit Himself, to empower us to be like Jesus. God has blessings and spiritual power in abundance for us. He is powerful and mighty and able to do what we can never do on our own.

God desires that we let the Holy Spirit flow through us in power to show people His love and to help people with His gifts. It all centers in Him.

God chooses the weak and foolish things of this world, on purpose, so that people may look at them and say, "It has to be God!"

GOD'S WORD FOR YOU

For we are not wrestling with flesh and blood
[contending only with physical opponents], but against
the despotisms, against the powers, against [the master
spirits who are] the world rulers of this present darkness,
against the spirit forces of wickedness in the heavenly
(supernatural) sphere.

EPHESIANS 6:12

THE WARFARE WITHIN

In waging spiritual warfare with God's power, we must remember that we war against Satan and his demons, not against other people . . . and not with our own selves.

Probably the greatest war we wage is one we wage with ourselves about ourselves, struggling with where we are spiritually compared to where we see we need to be. We may struggle with feeling that we should have accomplished more in life than we have; we may feel we are a financial failure or many other things. But one thing is a fact: We can't change anything by being frustrated and struggling within. Only God can fight our battles and win. These internal battles are truly battles and must be handled the same way the rest of our battles are.

It is difficult to get to the place where we can be honest with ourselves about our sin and failures, our inabilities and fallibilities, and yet still know that we are right with God because Jesus made us right when He died for us and rose from the dead. If you are at war within yourself, knowing you are right with God is a tremendous key to tapping into spiritual power.

❧

We can be changed as we worship and behold God —
not as we look at ourselves, adding up our many flaws —
but as we look to Him.

GOD'S WORD FOR YOU

But we all, with open face beholding as in a glass the glory of the Lord, are changed into the same image from glory to glory, even as by the Spirit of the Lord.

2 CORINTHIANS 3:18 KJV

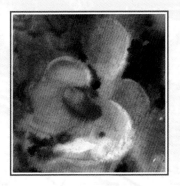

We Are Changing

I want to change, and I am sure you do also. I want to see changes in my behavior. I want to see regular progress. For example, I want more stability; I want to walk in a great measure of love and all the other fruit of the Spirit. I want to be kind and good to others, even if I don't feel good or am not having a particularly good day. Even when things are coming against me and things aren't working out the way I'd like, I still want to display the character of Jesus Christ.

Through the power of the Holy Spirit within us, we are able to be sweet, nice, and kind, even when things are not going our way. We are able to stay calm when everything around us seems topsy-turvy, when everything seems to be conspiring against us to cause us to lose our patience and get angry and upset.

The key for me has been to finally learn that God changes me through His grace, not through my struggles to change myself. I suffered many years of wrestling with myself before I discovered God's power to change me within—little by little.

This is how God changes us. He reveals something to us and then waits until we decide to trust Him with it before He works in us His character in that area.

GOD'S WORD FOR YOU

I am the Vine; you are the branches. Whoever lives in Me and I in him bears much (abundant) fruit. However, apart from Me [cut off from vital union with Me] you can do nothing.

JOHN 15:5

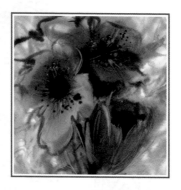

ONLY IN JESUS

I was a very independent person, and God began speaking John 15:5 to me early in my walk with Him. One of the spiritual laws of receiving spiritual power from God is entire dependence upon Him. Without faith we cannot please God. Faith involves the leaning of the entire human personality in absolute trust in God's power, wisdom, and goodness.

We are to lean on, rely only, and entirely depend on Him, taking all the weight off of ourselves and putting it all on Him. Without God's help, we can't change anything in our lives. We can't change ourselves, our spouse, our family, our friends, or our circumstances. Truly, apart from Him we cannot do anything!

We forfeit peace and joy when we fail to let God be God. We try to figure out things we have no business even touching with our minds. Nothing is too hard or too wonderful for God, but many things are too hard or too wonderful for us. We need to grow to the place where we rest in the fact that we know the One Who knows . . . and we're free to trust Him.

It is so liberating to say, "Lord, I don't know what to do, and even if I did, I couldn't do it. But my eyes are on You. I am going to wait and watch You work it all out."

GOD'S WORD FOR YOU

And all Judah stood before the Lord, with their children and their wives.

Then the Spirit of the Lord came upon Jahaziel son of Zechariah, the son of Benaiah, the son of Jeiel, the son of Mattaniah, a Levite of the sons of Asaph, in the midst of the assembly.

He said, Hearken, all Judah, you inhabitants of Jerusalem, and you King Jehoshaphat. The Lord says this to you: Be not afraid or dismayed at this great multitude; for the battle is not yours, but God's.

2 CHRONICLES 20:13–15

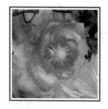

WAIT ON GOD

I love 2 Chronicles 20:13–15 because it is a power verse! King Jehoshaphat and the people were facing a vast army and impossible odds. But rather than take a natural action, Jehoshaphat took a spiritual action. In God's economy of spiritual power, waiting upon God and standing still is a spiritual action. In effect, he was saying, "Lord, I will wait upon You to deliver us. And I'm going to enjoy my life while I wait for You."

Satan hates our joy. He wants to see anger, unbridled emotions, tears, self-pity, grumbling, complaining, blaming God and others for our life situations. He wants to see anything but joy, because the joy of the Lord is our strength (Nehemiah 8:10). We need the strength we gain while waiting in order to do whatever it is God will instruct us to do when He gives us direction.

We are tempted to think we are not doing our part if we don't worry or try to figure out some answer, but this will prevent our deliverance rather than aid it. It is not irresponsible to enjoy life when we wait on the Lord to solve our problems (John 10:10).

God's answer was very plain and simple: Do not fear because the battle is not yours, but the Lord's.

GOD'S WORD FOR YOU

Tomorrow go down to them. Behold, they will come up by the Ascent of Ziz, and you will find them at the end of the ravine before the Wilderness of Jeruel.

You shall not need to fight in this battle; take your positions, stand still, and see the deliverance of the Lord [Who is] with you, O Judah and Jerusalem. Fear not nor be dismayed. Tomorrow go out against them, for the Lord is with you.

And Jehoshaphat bowed his head with his face to the ground, and all Judah and the inhabitants of Jerusalem fell down before the Lord, worshiping Him.

And some Levites of the Kohathites and Korahites stood up to praise the Lord, the God of Israel, with a very loud voice.

2 CHRONICLES 20:16–19

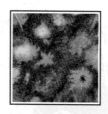

Take Your Position

The people of Judah did not only stand still before the Lord. When they heard the Lord's instruction, the king and the people bowed on their knees with their faces to the ground and worshiped. Wow! Worship was their actual position, and in worshiping they were also standing still. Kneeling in reverence before God is a battle position and a key to spiritual power.

To "praise" God means to ascribe to Him the glory due to His name. It means to talk about and sing out about the goodness, grace, and greatness of God. "To worship" is "to make obeisance, do reverence to, to serve." Broadly, it may be regarded as the direct acknowledgment to God, of His nature, attributes, ways, and claims, whether by the outgoing of the heart in praise and thanksgiving or by deed done in such an acknowledgment.

We must learn to fight God's way, not the world's way. Our battle position is one of worship. To stand means to abide or to enter God's rest. Our position in Christ is to worship and praise Him. We stand our ground and persist in believing that God will work in our life and circumstances. We refuse to give up.

*As we worship the Lord, we release the emotional
or mental burden that is weighing us down.
It is swallowed up in the awesomeness of God.*

GOD'S WORD FOR YOU

But those who wait for the Lord [who expect, look for, and hope in Him] shall change and renew their strength and power; they shall lift their wings and mount up [close to God] as eagles [mount up to the sun]; they shall run and not be weary, they shall walk and not faint or become tired.

ISAIAH 40:31

How Long, Lord?

By starting to worship God for the changes He is already working in us, we find that those changes start manifesting more and more. And we experience new levels of God's glory, which is the manifestation of all His excellencies. In other words, God will pour His goodness out upon the worshiper.

The amount of time the changes require in our lives is dependent upon (1) how long it takes us to get into agreement with God that we have the problem He says we have; (2) how long it takes us to stop making excuses and blaming it on someone else; (3) how long we spin our wheels, trying to change ourselves; (4) how much time we spend studying His Word, waiting on and worshiping Him, truly believing that He is working in us.

God is always trying to work in us. He calls Himself "I AM" and is ever present to change us. He is a gentleman and will not force His way into our lives; He must be invited. As we relax under His mighty hand, He begins to remold us into what His original intention was before the world messed us up. He will definitely do a good job, if we release ourselves into His mighty hand.

God can change you while you read this book, if you will trust Him.

GOD'S WORD FOR YOU

So Ahab went up to eat and to drink. And Elijah went up to the top of Carmel; and he bowed himself down upon the earth and put his face between his knees

And said to his servant, Go up now, look toward the sea. And he went up and looked and said, There is nothing. Elijah said, Go again seven times.

And at the seventh time the servant said, A cloud as small as a man's hand is arising out of the sea. And Elijah said, Go up, say to Ahab, Hitch your chariot and go down, lest the rain stop you.

In a little while, the heavens were black with wind-swept clouds, and there was a great rain. And Ahab went to Jezreel.

1 KINGS 18:42–45

26

RELEASING GOD

God changes us from one degree of glory to another, but don't forget to enjoy the glory you are in right now while you are headed for the next one. Don't compare the glory you are in with the glory of someone else who appears to be in a greater degree of glory. Each of us is an individual, and God deals with us differently, according to what He knows we need.

You may not notice changes on a daily basis, but I want to stir your faith up so you will believe that God is at work, just as He said He would be. Remember, we see *after* we believe, not *before*. We struggle with ourselves because of all that we are not, when we should be praising and worshiping God for all that we are. As we worship Him for Who He is, we see things released into our lives that we could have never made happen ourselves.

As we worship God, we are released from frustration. All those pent-up, weird, emotional things that need to go begin to vanish. As we worship, God's character is released in our lives and begins to manifest.

※

We release God to work in our lives as we release our faith in Him. God's truth will set you free if you stick with God's battle plan, and you will like the results!

GOD'S WORD FOR YOU

For those whom He foreknew [of whom He was aware and loved beforehand], He also destined from the beginning [foreordaining them] to be molded into the image of His Son [and share inwardly His likeness], that He might become the firstborn among many brethren.

ROMANS 8:29

And Jesus called [to Him] the throng with His disciples and said to them, If anyone intends to come after Me, let him deny himself [forget, ignore, disown, and lose sight of himself and his own interests] and take up his cross, and [joining Me as a disciple and siding with My party] follow with Me [continually, cleaving steadfastly to Me].

MARK 8:34

CHRISTLIKENESS

Our number one goal in life as Christians should be Christlikeness. Jesus is the express image of the Father, and we are to follow in His footsteps. He came as the Pioneer of our faith to show us by example how we should live. We should seek to behave with people the way Jesus did. Our goal is not to see how successful we can be in business or how famous we can be. It is not prosperity, popularity, or even building a big ministry, but to be Christlike.

Spiritual maturity or Christlikeness cannot be obtained without "dying to self." That simply means saying yes to God and no to ourselves when our will and God's are in opposition. Jesus told His disciples that if they wanted to follow Him, they would need to take up their cross daily.

To follow Christ and become like Him, we must be willing to forget about what we want—our plans, having our own way—and instead trust Him to show us what His will is for us. His will always leads to deep joy and satisfaction, and the prize is well worth it!

❧

The world is not impressed by our bumper stickers and Christian jewelry. They want to see fruit of godly behavior. They want to see lives energized by the Spirit of God that reflect the image of Jesus.

SUPERNATURAL FAVOR

The grace of God is the favor of God.
It is the supernatural power of God
coming through our faith to do what
we cannot do on our own.

GOD'S WORD FOR YOU

Let us then fearlessly and confidently and boldly draw near to the throne of grace (the throne of God's unmerited favor to us sinners), that we may receive mercy [for our failures] and find grace to help in good time for every need [appropriate help and well-timed help, coming just when we need it].

HEBREWS 4:16

Now to Him Who, by (in consequence of) the [action of His] power that is at work within us, is able to [carry out His purpose and] do superabundantly, far over and above all that we [dare] ask or think [infinitely beyond our highest prayers, desires, thoughts, hopes, or dreams] . . .

EPHESIANS 3:20

t w o

SUPERNATURAL FAVOR

hen I first started ministering, I was scared. I was afraid of being rejected. In those days, for a woman to do what I was doing was even less popular than it is today when women preachers are more widely accepted. So I bent over backward to speak and behave the way I thought was expected of me.

The problem was that I was trying to win natural favor, and it didn't and won't work. Trying to get favor on your own is not only hard work, it is often pointless. The harder you try, the less people are attracted to you.

At the time, I knew nothing about supernatural favor. I didn't know that favor is a part of grace. In fact, in the English New Testament the words *grace* and *favor* are both translated from the same Greek word *charis*. So the grace of God is the favor of God. And the grace of God causes things to happen in our life that need to happen, through the channel of our faith. It is the power of God coming through our faith to do what we cannot do on our own. It is not by human power, or by human might, but by the Holy Spirit that we receive favor. It is by God's Spirit of grace that we find favor with God and with man.

Once you believe God for supernatural favor, it relieves the stress that builds up in you. Rather than try to do everything for yourself, you just do your best and leave the results to God.

GOD'S WORD FOR YOU

But He gives us more and more grace (power of the Holy Spirit, to meet this evil tendency and all others fully). That is why He says, God sets Himself against the proud and haughty, but gives grace [continually] to the lowly (those who are humble enough to receive it).

JAMES 4:6

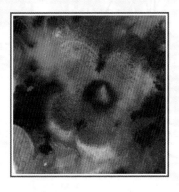

Natural Favor

I need to emphasize the distinction between natural favor and supernatural favor as it relates to spiritual power. Natural favor can be earned, whereas supernatural favor and power can't.

If you work hard enough and long enough, you can get people to like and accept you most of the time. But that acceptance must be maintained, and this is where so many people get into trouble. Saying and doing all the right things becomes a form of bondage.

God doesn't want us to spend our time and energy trying to earn favor with Him or with others. He wants us to devote our time and energy to walking in His supernatural favor through the Spirit and doing His will, whether it is popular or not. We cannot earn His favor; it is a pure gift from God. And the way we get it is simply by believing and receiving it from God.

This is why I pray daily for favor, supernatural favor. God gives grace to the humble, and it is my one desire that His spiritual power will freely flow through my life and words and actions.

❧

When we know that everything we have and enjoy is a gift from God, a result of His supernatural favor upon us, then there is nothing left for us to do but say, "Thank You, Lord."

GOD'S WORD FOR YOU

And Joseph's master took him and put him in the prison, a place where the state prisoners were confined; so he was there in the prison.

But the Lord was with Joseph, and showed him mercy and loving-kindness and gave him favor in the sight of the warden of the prison.

And the warden of the prison committed to Joseph's care all the prisoners who were in the prison; and whatsoever was done there, he was in charge of it.

The prison warden paid no attention to anything that was in [Joseph's] charge, for the Lord was with him and made whatever he did to prosper.

GENESIS 39:20–23

THE FAITH ATTITUDE

Although Joseph was being punished unfairly because he was jailed for something he didn't do, the Lord was still with him in supernatural favor and took care of him. He proved that a person is really not in too bad a shape, even if he ends up in prison, if God gives him favor.

No matter what happens to us in life, we can have favor with God and with other people (Luke 2:52). But like so many good things in life, just because something is available to us does not mean that we will partake of it. The Lord makes many things available to us that we never receive and enjoy because we never activate our faith in that area.

For example, if we go to a job interview confessing fear and failure, we will almost be assured not to get the job. On the other hand, even if we apply for a job that we know we aren't fully qualified for, we can still go in confidence, believing that God will give us favor in every situation that is His will.

God wants to give you favor, but you must do what Joseph did and believe for it. Joseph maintained a good attitude in a bad situation. He had a "faith attitude," and God gave him favor.

GOD'S WORD FOR YOU

Now when the turn for Esther the daughter of Abihail, the uncle of Mordecai who had taken her as his own daughter, had come to go in to the king, she required nothing but what Hegai the king's attendant, the keeper of the women, suggested. And Esther won favor in the sight of all who saw her.

So Esther was taken to King Ahasuerus into his royal palace in the tenth month, the month of Tebeth, in the seventh year of his reign.

And the king loved Esther more than all the women, and she obtained grace and favor in his sight more than all the maidens, so that he set the royal crown on her head and made her queen instead of Vashti.

ESTHER 2:15–17

Under God's Control

Did you know there is a Scripture that says God brings one person down and lifts up another? You need to read 1 Samuel 2:7. One instance is the life of Esther. God raised her up from obscurity to become the queen of the entire land. He gave her favor with everyone she met, including the king, because she had found favor with God.

Later in the story, Esther drew upon that favor to save herself and her people, the Jews, from being murdered by the evil Haman, who was out to destroy them. She may have been afraid to go to the king and ask him to intervene, because doing so could have cost her very life, but she did because she trusted her life to God.

Whatever situation comes into your life, even if you are being harassed, persecuted, or discriminated against, or someone is trying to take something from you that rightfully belongs to you—whether it is your job, your home, your reputation, or anything in life— believe God for supernatural favor. Despite how hopeless things may look, God can lift up and He can bring down. If your life is in His hands, believe that the light of the Lord shines upon you to give you favor.

Don't go through life being afraid or harboring a fear of rejection. God's power will always see you through.

GOD'S WORD FOR YOU

And the [Babylonian] king told Ashpenaz, the master of his eunuchs, to bring in some of the children of Israel, both of the royal family and of the nobility. . . .

Among these were of the children of Judah: Daniel, Hananiah, Mishael, and Azariah.

The chief of the eunuchs gave them names: Daniel he called Belteshazzar [the king's attendant], Hananiah he called Shadrach, Mishael he called Meshach, and Azariah he called Abednego.

But Daniel determined in his heart that he would not defile himself by [eating his portion of] the king's rich and dainty food or by [drinking] the wine which he drank; therefore he requested of the chief of the eunuchs that he might [be allowed] not to defile himself.

Now God made Daniel to find favor, compassion, and loving-kindness with the chief of the eunuchs.

DANIEL 1:3, 6–9

OVER AND ABOVE

The story of Daniel and the Hebrew children may be a familiar story, but we must not miss the lesson of how God's supernatural favor was with them after being taken far from their homes and families.

Because of their sins against the Lord, the nation of Judah was carried away into captivity in Babylon. There, some of the most promising of them, including Daniel and three of his friends, were chosen to become attendants to the Babylonian king. As part of their three-year period of training, these young men were to follow a diet of rich meat and wine provided from the king's table. However, Daniel and his friends determined not to defile themselves with this diet and asked to be allowed to follow their own Hebrew diet.

They refused to compromise their convictions, and we are told that the Lord gave Daniel "favor, compassion, and loving-kindness" with the chief of eunuchs. They had permission to follow their own diet as long as it didn't harm them. Of course, not only did it not harm them, it made them stronger and healthier and led them to be chosen as trusted counselors.

Under God's favor and power, Daniel rose to become prime minister of the world's greatest power. What would have happened if he had not trusted God over and above all he asked or imagined?

GOD'S WORD FOR YOU

And Jesus increased in wisdom (in broad and full understanding) and in stature and years, and in favor with God and man.

LUKE 2:52

Now the centurion, having seen what had taken place, recognized God and thanked and praised Him, and said, Indeed, without question, this Man was upright (just and innocent)!

LUKE 23:47

ℱAVORED OF THE LORD

From childhood, Jesus walked in the supernatural favor of God and men. In fact, once He began His public ministry, He was so popular that He could hardly find time to get alone to pray and fellowship with His heavenly Father. Even those who did not believe in Him recognized that He enjoyed the favor of God. When the Pharisees sent guards to arrest Jesus, they went back saying, "Never has a man talked as this Man talks!" (John 7:46). Right up until the very end of His life, even on the cross, that special favor and power were recognized (Luke 23:47–48).

That is the way I would like for you and me to come to see ourselves, as the favored of the Lord. He doesn't see us as weak, helpless, sinful creatures. He sees us robed in righteousness, shod with the shoes of peace, wearing the full armor of God, and wielding the sword of the Spirit, which is the Word of the Lord. That is how we ought to see ourselves.

No matter how we may appear to ourselves or to others, we must never forget that God can cause the light of His favor to shine upon us—just as He did for Jesus—so that we too increase in wisdom and stature.

Stop looking at your life in the natural. You are not giving the Lord any credit for what He can do.

GOD'S WORD FOR YOU

And I will pour out upon the house of David and upon the inhabitants of Jerusalem the Spirit of grace or unmerited favor and supplication.

ZECHARIAH 12:10

The Missing Link

The message of God's grace has been the single most important message that the Holy Spirit has ministered to me. My entire Christian experience was a struggle before I learned about the spiritual power of grace. To teach people faith and not teach them grace is, in my opinion, "the missing link" in many people's faith walk.

Grace is the power of the Holy Spirit that is available to do whatever needs to be done in our lives, the power to bring and sustain change. It is the ability of God that comes to us free for the asking. Through faith the grace of God is received. Faith is not the price that buys the blessings of God, but it is the hand that receives them.

Just hearing the word *grace* is soothing to me. Always remember that when you feel frustrated it is because you have entered into your own effort and need to get back into God's power. Grace leaves you strong and calm; works render you weak and powerless, frustrated and frantic. Don't be discouraged if change doesn't come as quickly as you'd like. It will take time.

Receive not only the grace that saves, but receive grace, grace, and more grace so you may live victoriously and glorify Jesus in your daily life.

GOD'S WORD FOR YOU

Now the Lord is the Spirit, and where the Spirit of the Lord is, there is liberty (emancipation from bondage, freedom).

2 CORINTHIANS 3:17

In [this] freedom Christ has made us free [and completely liberated us]; stand fast then, and do not be hampered and held ensnared and submit again to a yoke of slavery [which you have once put off].

GALATIANS 5:1

FREEDOM AND LIBERTY

Each of us would like to be favored or featured. Is that pride? No, not if that position comes from God and not from our own personal ambitions or our own selfish efforts to call attention to ourselves.

To be totally honest, I find it delightful to watch God feature a person. It is fun to watch Him single out someone for special attention or preferential treatment. To see Him work powerfully in someone's life provokes genuine praise and thanksgiving.

It is always enjoyable to have favor with God. It just seems that it doesn't happen as often as we would like. Part of the problem is us. We don't have nearly as much fun with the Lord as we should. We should have more freedom and liberty, and less fear and legalism. There are so many things that God would love to do for us, but He cannot because we won't ask. One reason we won't ask is because we don't feel worthy. The only time we will go to God and ask for special favor is when we are absolutely desperate.

It is time we believe the words of our Father: "You are the apple of My eye. You are My favorite child."

Our heavenly Father wants His children to stand up and be everything for which His Son, Jesus, gave His life that they might become.

GOD'S WORD FOR YOU

O Lord, our Lord, how excellent (majestic and glorious) is Your name in all the earth! You have set Your glory on [or above] the heavens.

Out of the mouths of babes and unweaned infants You have established strength because of Your foes, that You might silence the enemy and the avenger.

When I view and consider Your heavens, the work of Your fingers, the moon and the stars, which You have ordained and established,

What is man that You are mindful of him, and the son of [earthborn] man that You care for him?

Yet You have made him but a little lower than God [or heavenly beings], and You have crowned him with glory and honor.

You made him to have dominion over the works of Your hands; You have put all things under his feet . . .

PSALM 8:1–6

CROWNED WITH GLORY

If you notice in verse 5 of Psalm 8, God has chosen man and crowned him with glory and honor. Here, in my opinion, *honor* and *favor* have the same meaning. We might say that God has crowned man with glory and favor, giving him dominion over the works of His hand, and placing all things under his feet. I describe the word *glory* in this instance as the excellencies of God. And to be *crowned* symbolizes triumph and reward.

Just because we don't see a crown on our head doesn't mean there is none there. No matter what we feel, we have been crowned with God's favor and excellence. We were never meant to muddle our way through life, taking whatever the devil throws at us without claiming what is rightfully ours.

If you read verse 6, you will see that all things have been placed under our feet by God, Who has given us dominion over all His creation. By faith in the finished work of Jesus on the cross, we have all the spiritual power we need to prevent the devil and his demons from intimidating, dominating, and oppressing us. This is our right under God's favor.

*We walk in our God-given glory and honor
only to the extent we determine to do so.
Learn to avail yourself of it and walk in it.*

BE
TRANSFORMED

It is obvious that some people are closer to God than others. Some people have a "close friends" familiarity with God that seems foreign to others. The truth is that each of us is as close to God as we want to be.

GOD'S WORD FOR YOU

One thing have I asked of the Lord, that will I seek, inquire for, and [insistently] require: that I may dwell in the house of the Lord [in His presence] all the days of my life, to behold and gaze upon the beauty [the sweet attractiveness and the delightful loveliness] of the Lord and to meditate, consider, and inquire in His temple.

PSALM 27:4

three

BE TRANSFORMED

remember the emptiness I felt in 1976 when as a young Christian I realized that doing the right things brought temporary happiness but not deep, satisfying joy. My relationship with God was much like the Israelites', who could only see God from a distance while Moses talked with God face-to-face. God was very real to them, and they could hear His voice, but to them He looked like a consuming fire.

Perhaps you are experiencing what I went through. I lived by the law of the church, doing everything I was told to do, and expecting my routine of good works to bring the peace and joy and spiritual power the Scriptures promise. Instead, I found myself deeply disheartened that nothing seemed to be working. My life was full of irritations and aggravations that robbed me of true contentment. I knew I needed real change in my life, but I didn't know what I needed. I was searching, but I didn't know what I was searching for.

Many of us want the blessings and power of God, but we don't crave and pursue Him, or lay aside other things to go after a word from the Lord. We want to be transformed, but unlike David, we fail to commit ourselves to one thing—the manifest presence of God.

The only thing that truly satisfies the longing within is to know God more intimately today than we did yesterday.

GOD'S WORD FOR YOU

But He replied, It has been written, Man shall not live and be upheld and sustained by bread alone, but by every word that comes forth from the mouth of God.

MATTHEW 4:4

And do not get drunk with wine, for that is debauchery; but ever be filled and stimulated with the [Holy] Spirit.

EPHESIANS 5:18

A REALITY CHECK

I don't think there's anything better than just to be satisfied. To wake up in the morning and think, *Life is good, praise God, I'm satisfied,* and to go to bed at night still satisfied is truly living abundantly. On the other hand, I don't think there is anything much worse than living in a low-level state of dissatisfaction all the time.

Here is a spiritual reality check. No matter what you own, where you go, or what you do, nothing can give you true gratification besides the presence of God. Money, trips, vacations, clothes, new opportunities, new furniture and new houses, getting married and having children are all things that can give us a degree of happiness. But we will never be permanently, consistently satisfied if we seek things to own or do in order to quench the empty void inside us.

I am pressing this point because I know there are many unhappy believers who are without the knowledge of what to do about their dry, unfulfilled lives. Too many are missing out on the rich pleasure that comes from fellowshipping daily with the heavenly Father through the Holy Spirit. If that's true in your life, be honest with God and open your heart to Him.

If we are ever to have real victory,
you and I have to learn the simple scriptural truth:
We have not because we ask not.

GOD'S WORD FOR YOU

So I say to you, Ask and keep on asking and it shall be given you; seek and keep on seeking and you shall find; knock and keep on knocking and the door shall be opened to you.

For everyone who asks and keeps on asking receives; and he who seeks and keeps on seeking finds; and to him who knocks and keeps on knocking, the door shall be opened.

What father among you, if his son asks for a loaf of bread, will give him a stone; or if he asks for a fish, will instead of a fish give him a serpent?

Or if he asks for an egg, will give him a scorpion?

If you then, evil as you are, know how to give good gifts [gifts that are to their advantage] to your children, how much more will your heavenly Father give the Holy Spirit to those who ask and continue to ask Him!

LUKE 11:9–13

FILLED WITH THE SPIRIT

On a Friday morning in February 1976, I was driving to work and feeling discouraged. Nothing in my life seemed to be working right, despite my best attempts. Out of sheer frustration and desperation I cried out to God that I couldn't go on any longer with the way things were. I was like a starving person, so spiritually hungry I was ready to receive anything as long as I knew it was from God. I was totally open to God.

To my surprise God spoke to me in the car that morning. He called my name and spoke to me about patience. I knew with certainty that God was going to do something in my life, although I didn't know what He would do or when.

After work, I was sitting at a red light, and I felt my heart fill with faith about what God was going to do. I began to thank Him for it, and at that very moment, Jesus filled me with the presence of the Holy Spirit in a way I had never experienced. It felt as if someone had poured me full of liquid love, and it had such a profound effect upon my behavior that people began asking me what had happened. I was peaceful, happy, and easy to get along with—truly changed!

We are to seek the Lord, and not the experience of another person. He alone decides how and exactly when to manifest His presence in our lives.

GOD'S WORD FOR YOU

And having said this, He breathed on them and said to them, Receive the Holy Spirit!

JOHN 20:22

And while being in their company and eating at the table with them, He commanded them not to leave Jerusalem but to wait for what the Father had promised, Of which [He said] you have heard Me speak.

For John baptized with water, but not many days from now you shall be baptized with (placed in, introduced into) the Holy Spirit. . . .

But you shall receive power (ability, efficiency, and might) when the Holy Spirit has come upon you, and you shall be My witnesses in Jerusalem and all Judea and Samaria and to the ends (the very bounds) of the earth.

ACTS 1:4–5, 8

Immersed in the Spirit

Before Jesus was taken up into heaven after He was resurrected from the dead (Acts 1:3), He gathered the disciples and told them not to leave Jerusalem but to wait for the coming outpouring of the Holy Spirit. These were the same disciples whom Jesus had previously breathed upon and told to receive the Holy Spirit. I believe this was when they were born again. So if the disciples had already received the Holy Spirit, which they had, why were they told to await the baptism of the Holy Spirit?

When we are born again, we have the Holy Spirit *in* us. Acts 1:8 promises that He will also come *upon* us with power to be Christ's witnesses to the ends of the earth. Not only do we enjoy the indwelling presence of God's Spirit through salvation, but we can receive His power to fill us in order to demonstrate His glory to the lost people around us.

A person may have a desire to do something and yet not have the power to perform it. In my life, it was only after I had been immersed in the Holy Spirit that I found the true desire to do God's will and the power to do it. It's the difference between doing and being.

There are countless things we struggle with when we could be receiving help from the divine Helper.

GOD'S WORD FOR YOU

Then Jesus came from Galilee to the Jordan to John to be baptized by him. . . .

And when Jesus was baptized, He went up at once out of the water; and behold, the heavens were opened, and he [John] saw the Spirit of God descending like a dove and alighting on Him.

MATTHEW 3:13, 16

How God anointed and consecrated Jesus of Nazareth with the [Holy] Spirit and with strength and ability and power; how He went about doing good and, in particular, curing all who were harassed and oppressed by [the power of] the devil, for God was with Him.

ACTS 10:38

ANOINTED WITH THE SPIRIT

Although Jesus was Himself God Who became flesh (John 1:1–14), we know that He laid aside His divine privileges to assume the guise of a servant in that He became like men and was born a human being (Philippians 2:6–7). Then He demonstrated the steps He wanted us to follow.

Before Jesus' public ministry began, He was anointed with the Holy Spirit and power. The description of the Holy Spirit's descent upon Jesus indicates that the Spirit permanently remained with Him (John 1:32).

For the Holy Spirit to reside with Jesus is significant because under the Old Covenant the Spirit came upon people for specific tasks but did not permanently remain on them. After the Spirit's descent, Jesus was led by the Spirit to be tempted by the devil and passed every test. Then He began His preaching ministry, which included miracles and other mighty acts empowered by the Holy Spirit.

When you are filled with the Holy Spirit, you are equipped for service in the kingdom of God. You receive the power that enables you to do what God wants you to do.

If Jesus needed to be baptized by the Holy Spirit, don't we need the same?

GOD'S WORD FOR YOU

Then he fell to the ground, and heard a voice saying to him, "Saul, Saul, why are you persecuting Me?"

And he said, "Who are You, Lord?" Then the Lord said, "I am Jesus, whom you are persecuting. It is hard for you to kick against the goads."

So he, trembling and astonished, said, "Lord, what do You want me to do?" Then the Lord said to him, "Arise and go into the city, and you will be told what you must do."

ACTS 9:4–6 NKJV

So Ananias left and went into the house. And he laid his hands on Saul and said, Brother Saul, the Lord Jesus, Who appeared to you along the way by which you came here, has sent me that you may recover your sight and be filled with the Holy Spirit.

ACTS 9:17

THE TRANSFORMATION OF PAUL

Many say that believers receive everything they will ever get or need when they accept Jesus as Savior. That may be the case with some believers, but certainly not all. Different people have different experiences. I am not denying that some may be born again and baptized with the Holy Spirit at the same time; but others are not, and Paul was one of them.

When Paul (formerly called Saul) encountered the glorified Christ on the road to Damascus (Acts 9), he was persecuting Christians at the time, believing he was doing God a service. This was the moment of Paul's conversion, the time of his surrender as he called Jesus "Lord" and obeyed His instructions.

Three days later, the Lord spoke to a disciple named Ananias in a vision to go and pray for Paul. Despite the evil Paul had done, Ananias is told that Paul is a chosen instrument to bring the Gospel to the Gentiles and descendants of Israel. When Ananias laid his hands on Paul, Paul's eyes were opened, he was filled with the Holy Spirit, and then he went to be baptized in water. To say that his life changed forever at that moment is an understatement.

If the apostle Paul needed to be filled with the Holy Spirit, don't we need the same?

GOD'S WORD FOR YOU

[That you may really come] to know [practically, through experience for yourselves] the love of Christ, which far surpasses mere knowledge [without experience]; that you may be filled [through all your being] unto all the fullness of God [may have the richest measure of the divine Presence, and become a body wholly filled and flooded with God Himself]!

EPHESIANS 3:19

RECEIVING THE HOLY SPIRIT

I've focused on the baptism of the Holy Spirit because it is your personal key to spiritual power. Reading all this information will be of very little value to you unless you receive the Holy Spirit into your life. Spiritual power is an empty concept apart from Him.

To be filled with the Spirit, we must first have a desire. I believe that God often does not answer our first cries because He wants us to get desperate enough to be totally open to whatever He wants to do in our life. If you are truly hungry for more of God in your life, you are a candidate for the Spirit's baptism.

Receiving the Holy Spirit in our life is a holy thing, to be reverenced and even feared in a respectful way. God does not endue us with His power just for fun and games. He is a God of purpose, and all that He does in our life is for a purpose. Finding God's purpose and allowing Him to equip us for it should be the primary quest in our lives.

If you have this holy desire, God will meet you where you are. Open the door of your heart by stretching your faith out to God. Humble yourself and be prepared to obey whatever God asks of you.

Answer that knock at your heart's door and allow the Holy Spirit to come into your life in all His fullness.

GOD'S WORD FOR YOU

You do not have, because you do not ask.

JAMES 4:2

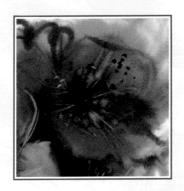

ASK AND RECEIVE

If you have read this far, it is now time to ask. Remember, the Holy Spirit will fill you, but only if invited to do so (Luke 11:13). Come boldly and ask. Ask fully expecting to receive. Don't be double-minded. Don't listen to doubt. Ask in faith. Believe you will receive, and you will receive. God is not a man that He should lie. He is faithful to fulfill His Word.

I had a definite experience of feeling the Spirit being poured into me. Since then, I have ministered the baptism of the Holy Spirit to literally thousands of people, and I have seen people react in every way. Many people do not feel a thing. Our experience cannot be based on feelings, but rather on faith.

Here is a prayer you might want to use: "Father, in Jesus' name, I ask You to baptize me in the power of the Holy Spirit with the evidence of speaking in tongues. Grant me boldness as You did those who were filled on the Day of Pentecost and give me other gifts that You desire me to have. Amen."

Wait on God quietly and believe that you are receiving. Don't try to make something happen. Let God minister to your spirit. To speak in tongues, open your mouth, and as the Spirit gives you utterance, speak forth what you hear coming up from your spirit. Give yourself totally to the Lord and trust Him as never before.

GOD'S WORD FOR YOU

And when the day of Pentecost had fully come, they were all assembled together in one place,

When suddenly there came a sound from heaven like the rushing of a violent tempest blast, and it filled the whole house in which they were sitting.

And there appeared to them tongues resembling fire, which were separated and distributed and which settled on each one of them.

And they were all filled (diffused throughout their souls) with the Holy Spirit and began to speak in other (different, foreign) languages (tongues), as the Spirit kept giving them clear and loud expression [in each tongue in appropriate words].

ACTS 2:1–4

EVIDENCE OF THE BAPTISM

The most important evidences of the Spirit-filled life are a character change and the development of the fruit of the Holy Spirit. Man is baptized by the Holy Spirit to enable him to live fully for God. Speaking in tongues was one of the evidences at Pentecost, but the most important evidence then was, and always will be, changed men and women.

The baptism of the Spirit changed Peter suddenly from a fearful man into an incredibly bold man. It transformed all the disciples of Jesus. We've already seen its effect in the life of Paul. It changed me, and it continues to change earnest seekers the world over.

Speaking in tongues is also an evidence, and it is a very valuable gift. I believe that the first outpouring on the Day of Pentecost is a pattern for the church to follow, and *all* of them spoke with other tongues.

I believe many people are baptized with the Holy Spirit and don't speak in tongues. I don't believe it is because they can't, but perhaps because they have been taught not to or perhaps they don't want the stigma that has unfortunately been attached to this gift. I beg you not to be afraid of God's good gift.

Outer power only comes from inner purity
that transforms us into new men and women.

LIFE IN THE SPIRIT

*If you truly want to experience
the life of the Spirit as God intended,
then you must continually open every area
of your heart for Him to keep transforming
you by His power.*

GOD'S WORD FOR YOU

And we are setting these truths forth in words not taught by human wisdom but taught by the [Holy] Spirit, combining and interpreting spiritual truths with spiritual language [to those who possess the Holy Spirit].

1 CORINTHIANS 2:13

four

LIFE IN THE SPIRIT

was taught that the baptism in the Holy Spirit, speaking in tongues and the other gifts of the Spirit, and signs and wonders had passed away with the early church. Sadly, that is almost an accurate statement, but that was never God's will, nor His intention. He has always had a remnant of people somewhere in the earth who still believe in everything the Bible teaches, and it has been through that remnant that He has kept the truth alive.

If you have been one of the people who have not believed in these things, please read on and examine for yourself the Word of God. Most people are a little afraid of things they don't understand. We don't understand the supernatural realm, yet we are created by God in such a way that we hunger for it. We all have an interest in the supernatural, and if our need is not met by God, Satan will attempt to give us a counterfeit.

God gave me an awesome experience with the baptism in the Holy Spirit, and I was filled to overflowing. That was over twenty-five years ago, and I have never been the same since. God will do the same for you if you ask Him.

Life in the Spirit will bring you a closer fellowship and intimacy with God than you have ever known before.

GOD'S WORD FOR YOU

*And afterward I will pour out My Spirit upon all flesh;
and your sons and your daughters shall prophesy, your old
men shall dream dreams, your young men shall see visions.*

*Even upon the menservants and upon the maidservants
in those days will I pour out My Spirit.*

JOEL 2:28–29

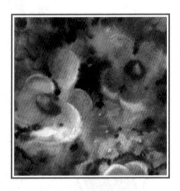

LIFE UNDER THE NEW COVENANT

The Old Covenant was a covenant of works, based on doing everything ourselves—struggling, striving, and laboring to be acceptable to God. It leaves us trapped in the works of the flesh. That kind of covenant steals our joy and peace.

But remember that the New Covenant is a covenant of grace, which is not based on what we can do, but what Christ has already done for us. Therefore, we are justified by our faith, not our works. That is so wonderful because it takes the pressure off us to perform. We can give up our outward efforts and allow God to work through us by the power of His Holy Spirit within us.

The bottom line is, the Old Covenant brings us bondage; the New Covenant brings us liberty. The infilling with the Holy Spirit is different from anything else we may experience. It enables us to *be* what we are supposed to be for God and then *do* what we are supposed to do.

Life in the Spirit is an awesome journey of living in the presence of God and being satisfied with God Himself.

God wants to bring a refreshing into your life, like a mighty wind. Don't be poverty-stricken in your soul when the answer is living inside you.

GOD'S WORD FOR YOU

For it is by free grace (God's unmerited favor) that you are saved (delivered from judgment and made partakers of Christ's salvation) through [your] faith. And this [salvation] is not of yourselves [of your own doing, it came not through your own striving], but it is the gift of God;

Not because of works [not the fulfillment of the Law's demands], lest any man should boast. [It is not the result of what anyone can possibly do, so no one can pride himself in it or take glory to himself.]

EPHESIANS 2:8–9

THE SPIRIT OF GRACE

Hebrews 10:29 tells us that it is "the [Holy] Spirit [Who imparts] grace (the unmerited favor and blessing of God)."

Grace is the power of the Holy Spirit available to you to do with ease what you cannot do by striving. But first, it is the power that enables you to be right with God so that you will become His home, the home of the Holy Spirit. With the Holy Spirit inside you, you can reach *in* to draw on the power of the Spirit of grace to do what you cannot do by striving in your own power.

The Holy Spirit ministers grace to us from God the Father. Grace is actually the Holy Spirit's power flowing out from the throne of God toward people to save them and enable them to live holy lives and accomplish the will of God.

There is no rejoicing in life without grace. With the grace of God, life can be lived with an effortless ease that produces an abundance of peace and joy.

❧

When God makes the changes, God gets the glory. He won't let us change ourselves. We simply need to ask Him to change us and let His grace do its work in us.

GOD'S WORD FOR YOU

*If you are censured and suffer abuse [because you bear]
the name of Christ, blessed [are you—happy, fortunate,
to be envied, with life-joy, and satisfaction in God's favor
and salvation, regardless of your outward condition],
because the Spirit of glory, the Spirit of God, is resting
upon you. On their part He is blasphemed, but on your
part He is glorified.*

1 PETER 4:14

THE SPIRIT OF GLORY

Peter states that the Spirit of God, the Spirit of glory, rests upon us when we are reproached for the Name of Christ. We think it is awful when people mistreat us because we are Christians, but God sees it in an entirely different light. God never expects us to suffer for Him without His help. We can firmly believe that any time we are reproached or mistreated in any way because of our faith in Christ, God gives us an extra measure of His Spirit to counterbalance the attack. There is power to overcome.

When we have the Spirit of God in our lives, we can go through difficult circumstances and keep our peace and joy. Like Shadrach, Meshach, and Abednego in Daniel 3:21–27, we can go into the fiery furnace, or into problems and struggles, and come out without even the smell of smoke upon us.

When God's glory is manifested in your life, others will look at you and say, "Wow, what a great God you serve," because the power of His goodness toward you is visually evident to them. God wants to "Wow" you and them even more!

Welcome the Spirit of glory into your life and get excited about seeing the glory of God rise upon you in your difficult circumstances of life.

GOD'S WORD FOR YOU

Thus it is written, The first man Adam became a living being (an individual personality); the last Adam (Christ) became a life-giving Spirit [restoring the dead to life].

But it is not the spiritual life which came first, but the physical and then the spiritual.

The first man [was] from out of earth, made of dust (earthly-minded); the second Man [is] the Lord from out of heaven.

Now those who are made of the dust are like him who was first made of the dust (earthly-minded); and as is [the Man] from heaven, so also [are those] who are of heaven (heavenly-minded).

And just as we have borne the image [of the man] of dust, so shall we and so let us also bear the image [of the Man] of heaven.

1 CORINTHIANS 15:45–49

THE SPIRIT OF LIFE

When God created Adam, he lay on the ground a lifeless form until God breathed into him the breath of life, and he became a living soul. First Corinthians 15:45 says, "The first man Adam became a living being (an individual personality). . . ." Adam walked beside God, talked to Him, and believed in Him.

That verse goes on to say that Jesus, "the last Adam (Christ) became a life-giving Spirit [restoring the dead to life]." God gives us a physical life first, and then a spiritual. This spiritual rebirth is given to those who place their trust in God, believing that Jesus paid the price for sin and died for those who sincerely repent of their sins, change their minds for the better, and amend their ways.

When we accept Christ as our Savior, the Spirit of life comes to dwell within us, and we are quickened and made alive in our spirit. He has come that we may experience a life filled with the power of the Spirit of God, or a heavenly minded life as the life Jesus lived.

Jesus is the Light of the World, and His Spirit is the Spirit of life that swallows up death and all that tries to defeat us.

GOD'S WORD FOR YOU

But when He, the Spirit of Truth (the Truth-giving Spirit) comes, He will guide you into all the Truth (the whole, full Truth). For He will not speak His own message [on His own authority]; but He will tell whatever He hears [from the Father; He will give the message that has been given to Him], and He will announce and declare to you the things that are to come [that will happen in the future].

JOHN 16:13

THE SPIRIT OF TRUTH

In John 16:13, Jesus Himself refers to the Holy Spirit as the Spirit of Truth. The Holy Spirit was sent to guide us into all truth after Jesus' departure into heaven after His death, burial, and resurrection. In the previous verse, Jesus told His disciples, "I have still many things to say to you, but you are not able to bear them or to take them upon you or to grasp them now." He told them that the Holy Spirit would continue revealing things to them as they became ready to receive them.

We live in a world today that is filled with people who are living false lives, wearing masks of pretense and hiding things. That is wrong. But the reason it happens is that people have not been taught how to walk in the truth. You don't have to be afraid of truth. God won't bring revelation to you by His Spirit until He knows you are ready.

When the Spirit of Truth convicts us of sin, we need to turn that word back to Him and depend upon Him to give us the power to change it. The key to holiness is not pressure to perform but power to live.

If you are brave enough and wise enough to welcome the Spirit of Truth into every area of your life, you are in for a journey that you will never forget.

GOD'S WORD FOR YOU

So too the [Holy] Spirit comes to our aid and bears us up in our weakness; for we do not know what prayer to offer nor how to offer it worthily as we ought, but the Spirit Himself goes to meet our supplication and pleads in our behalf with unspeakable yearnings and groanings too deep for utterance.

And He Who searches the hearts of men knows what is in the mind of the [Holy] Spirit [what His intent is], because the Spirit intercedes and pleads [before God] in behalf of the saints according to and in harmony with God's will.

ROMANS 8:26–27

THE SPIRIT OF SUPPLICATION

According to Zechariah 12:10, the Holy Spirit is the Spirit of supplication. That means He is the Spirit of prayer. Each time we sense a desire to pray, it is the Holy Spirit giving us the desire. We may not realize how often the Holy Spirit is leading us to pray. We may just wonder why we have a certain person or situation on our mind so much. We frequently think of someone, and instead of praying, we keep thinking.

Recognizing when we are being led by the Holy Spirit to pray is often a lesson that takes a long time to learn. This is because we attribute far too many things to coincidence or chance rather than realizing that God is attempting to lead us by His Spirit.

When God gives us a burden to pray for someone, He wants to use us as His ministers and representatives, but we must learn to be more sensitive to the Spirit of supplication. The Holy Spirit not only leads us to pray, He helps us to pray. He shows us how to pray when we don't know what to pray for.

Welcome the Spirit of supplication into your life and allow the ministry of prayer to be fulfilled through you. It is quite wonderful to watch the miraculous things that take place in response to prayer.

GOD'S WORD FOR YOU

For [the Spirit which] you have now received [is] not a spirit of slavery to put you once more in bondage to fear, but you have received the Spirit of adoption [the Spirit producing sonship] in [the bliss of] which we cry, Abba (Father)! Father!

ROMANS 8:15

But God—so rich is He in His mercy! Because of and in order to satisfy the great and wonderful and intense love with which He loved us,

Even when we were dead (slain) by [our own] shortcomings and trespasses, He made us alive together in fellowship and in union with Christ; [He gave us the very life of Christ Himself, the same new life with which He quickened Him, for] it is by grace (His favor and mercy which you did not deserve) that you are saved (delivered from judgment and made partakers of Christ's salvation).

EPHESIANS 2:4–5

THE SPIRIT OF ADOPTION

The apostle Paul teaches us that the Holy Spirit is the Spirit of adoption. The word *adoption* means that we are brought into the family of God, even though we were previously outsiders, unrelated to God in any way. We were sinners serving Satan, but God in His great mercy redeemed us and purchased us with the blood of His own Son.

We understand adoption in the natural sense. We know that some children without parents are adopted by people who purposely choose them and take them as their own. What an honor to be chosen on purpose by those who want to pour out their love on them.

This is exactly what God did for us as believers in Christ. Because of what Jesus did for us on the cross, we are now eternally part of His family, and His Spirit dwells in our spirit and cries out to the Father. God the Father decided before the foundation of the world was laid that anyone who loved Christ would be loved and accepted by Him as His child. He decided He would adopt all those who accepted Jesus as their Savior. We become heirs of God and joint heirs with His Son, Jesus Christ.

It is the knowledge of our family relationship to God that gives us boldness to go before His throne and let our requests be made known.

GOD'S WORD FOR YOU

And [as to His divine nature] according to the Spirit of holiness was openly designated the Son of God in power [in a striking, triumphant and miraculous manner] by His resurrection from the dead, even Jesus Christ our Lord (the Messiah, the Anointed One).

ROMANS 1:4

THE SPIRIT OF HOLINESS

The Holy Spirit is called that because He is the holiness of God and because it is His job to work that holiness in all those who believe in Jesus Christ as Savior.

In 1 Peter 1:15–16, we are told: "But as the One Who called you is holy, you yourselves also be holy in all your conduct and manner of living. For it is written, You shall be holy, for I am holy." God would never tell us to be holy without giving us the help we need to make us that way. An unholy spirit could never make us holy, so God sends His Holy Spirit into our heart to do a complete and thorough work in us. The Holy Spirit will continue to work in us as long as we are on this earth. God hates sin, and anytime He finds it in us, He quickly works to cleanse us of it.

The Holy Spirit is also the Spirit of judgment and of burning, which relates to His being the Spirit of holiness. He judges sin in us and burns it out of us. It is not pleasant work as far as our feelings are concerned, but it eventually brings us into the state God desires us to be so that we may glorify Him.

Don't be a compromising Christian who has one foot in the world and one foot in the kingdom of God. Rather, be on fire for God, allowing His Spirit of holiness to refine you as pure gold.

CHANGED INTO HIS LIKENESS

We are to be living epistles read
of all men. We are to be lights shining
out brightly in a dark world. In order
to do that, we have to be people
of integrity, people of character,
people molded into the image of Jesus.

GOD'S WORD FOR YOU

God said, Let Us [Father, Son, and Holy Spirit] make mankind in Our image, after Our likeness, and let them have complete authority over the fish of the sea, the birds of the air, the [tame] beasts, and over all of the earth, and over everything that creeps upon the earth.

GENESIS 1:26

My little children, for whom I am again suffering birth pangs until Christ is completely and permanently formed (molded) within you . . .

GALATIANS 4:19

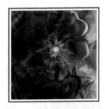

five

CHANGED INTO HIS LIKENESS

hen God said, "Let Us make man in Our image," this image does not refer to a physical likeness, but to character likeness. He meant that we were going to take on His nature, His character, as reflected in His Son, Jesus. It is to the degree that we are transformed into His image and likeness that spiritual power flows into and through our lives to the world around us.

The greatest goal of every believer should be Christlikeness. It is our highest calling in life. We should want the spiritual power within our lives to be able to handle situations the way Jesus would handle them and to treat people the way He would treat them. We should want to do things the way He would do them.

Jesus is our example. In John 13:15, He told His disciples, after washing their feet as a servant, "For I have given you this as an example, so that you should do [in your turn] what I have done to you." Peter tells us in 1 Peter 2:21: "For even to this were you called [it is inseparable from your vocation]. For Christ also suffered for you, leaving you [His personal] example, so that you should follow in His footsteps." May we humble ourselves as we seek to follow in those magnificent footsteps.

God is going to keep working with each of us until we get to the place where we act the way Jesus would act in every situation in life.

GOD'S WORD FOR YOU

And I am convinced and sure of this very thing, that He Who began a good work in you will continue until the day of Jesus Christ [right up to the time of His return], developing [that good work] and perfecting and bringing it to full completion in you.

PHILIPPIANS 1:6

Molded into His Image

According to the Bible, God is the Potter, and we are the clay (Romans 9:20–21). We are like a hard, cold lump of clay that is not very pliable or easy to work with. But He puts us on His potter's wheel and begins to refashion and remake us because He doesn't like what we have become.

Sometimes that process of molding is very painful to us. The reason it hurts so much is that we do not fit the mold into which God is trying to fit us. So God keeps working and working on us, trimming away this bad attitude and that wrong mind-set, carefully remolding and reshaping us until gradually we are changed into the likeness of His Son.

Don't be discouraged with yourself because you have not yet arrived. You can walk in spiritual power as long as you maintain an attitude of pressing on. As long as you do your best to cooperate with God, He is pleased with you. Enjoy your life in the Spirit right now on the way to where God is shaping you. Let the Potter do His work of changing you from glory to glory.

❧

God does not want us to be moldy; He wants us to be molded. Molded into the image of His Son. Remember, God will be shaping us right up until the time that Jesus returns to the earth!

GOD'S WORD FOR YOU

Moreover [let us also be full of joy now!] let us exult
and triumph in our troubles and rejoice in our sufferings,
knowing that pressure and affliction and hardship produce
patient and unswerving endurance.

And endurance (fortitude) develops maturity of
character (approved faith and tried integrity). And
character [of this sort] produces [the habit of] joyful and
confident hope of eternal salvation.

Such hope never disappoints or deludes or shames us,
for God's love has been poured out in our hearts through
the Holy Spirit Who has been given to us.

ROMANS 5:3–5

CHARACTER DEVELOPMENT

God wants to restore all of our character to godliness. Habit is actually character.

Habits are formed by discipline or the lack of discipline. Our character is basically what we do over and over. It is what other people have come to expect of us, such as being on time or how we respond in a certain circumstance. They know they can count or not count on us in this area. Over time, habits become part of our character.

We should not get legalistic about our character issues, but we do need to make an effort to develop character in those areas where we know we have problems. Changes in character come about by developing new habits. We need to commit ourselves to changing these faulty habits every time we confront them.

Godly character has much to do with discipline and the habits we form. Just as you can develop the habit of being on time, you can develop the habit of listening or giving to other people. You can choose to be kind and gentle, to curtail your spending, to watch your words, to pray, and to give thanks. It's about all of your life being shaped into the image of Christ.

God's power flows through faithful people, those who are faithful in the wilderness as well as the Promised Land.

GOD'S WORD FOR YOU

*He was guilty of no sin, neither was deceit (guile)
ever found on His lips.*

*When He was reviled and insulted, He did not revile
or offer insult in return; [when] He was abused and suffered,
He made no threats [of vengeance]; but he trusted [Himself
and everything] to Him Who judges fairly.*

1 PETER 2:22–23

CHARISMA IS NOT CHARACTER

According to Webster, one definition of *charisma* is "great personal magnetism: CHARM," but *character* is "moral or ethical strength: INTEGRITY." There are a lot of people who have charisma, but no character. Many people have a charming gift that can take them places where their character cannot keep them. We see this all the time in life and in the church.

Our character is revealed by what we do when nobody is watching. This was a key issue in my life and is a key to walking in spiritual power with God. Many people will do the right thing when somebody is watching them, but they won't do the right thing when nobody sees but God. As Christians, our commitment should be, "I am going to do the right thing simply because it is right."

Character is also seen when we do the right thing to others even though the right thing is not yet happening to us. As demonstrated by Jesus, one test of our character is, will we treat somebody right who is not treating us right? Will we bless someone who is not blessing us? It all comes down to what's in our heart, whether we trust Him Who judges fairly.

❧

Our character is seen in how much strength we have to do the right thing even when we don't want to do it.

GOD'S WORD FOR YOU

The integrity of the upright shall guide them, but the willful contrariness and crookedness of the treacherous shall destroy them.

PROVERBS 11:3

Arise [from the depression and prostration in which circumstances have kept you—rise to a new life]! Shine (be radiant with the glory of the Lord), for your light has come, and the glory of the Lord has risen upon you!

For behold, darkness shall cover the earth, and dense darkness [all] peoples, but the Lord shall arise upon you [O Jerusalem], and His glory shall be seen on you.

ISAIAH 60:1–2

PERSONAL INTEGRITY

We live in a society that has so lost its sense of moral values that common decency is often not even practiced. Our world no longer honors God and is not concerned about integrity. Whether it involves cheating or committing fraud or speaking half-truths and exaggerations that lead others to believe something that is not true, our culture is saturated with the lies of the enemy.

As believers, we live in the world but are not to be of the world (John 17:11, 14). If we want to walk in spiritual power, we cannot compromise our integrity and act as the world does. *Integrity* is "a firm adherence to a code or standard of values." Our code is the Word of God. There are certain things we wouldn't even think of doing, but there are too many compromises, even in the lives of God's people. There are things we do that Jesus would not do, and He is our standard of integrity.

Integrity is being committed to a life of excellence, as our God is excellent. It is doing the right thing every time, no matter what it costs us.

In the body of Christ, we must guard against having leaves without the fruit (Matthew 21:9)—counterfeit spirituality, empty talk, and lifeless formulas.

GOD'S WORD FOR YOU

Depart from evil and do good; seek, inquire for, and crave peace and pursue (go after) it!

PSALM 34:14

The Power of Peace

David instructs us to pursue peace, to crave and go after it. If we want to be in the flow of God's power, it's never going to happen if we are constantly frustrated and stressed out in our lives. If that is true of your life, you may need to cut a few things out of your life.

If you want the peace of God to permeate your life, you cannot exceed your limits. Nobody says you have to do all the things you are doing. Start looking at your life, figure out the commitments that are not bearing any fruit, and start pruning them. You are the one who makes your schedule, and you are the only one who can change it.

It is so important not to overcommit yourself. You need to follow God's leading as to what you are involved in and where you are to use your energy. That includes commitments to your children. Kids don't have to do everything they want to do, and they can't be allowed to control you and your family.

Satan will work overtime to get us to lose our peace and take us away from our faith. Rest in the assurance that God is with us in all that we face.

We must learn to say yes when God says yes and no when He says no. Only as we are obedient to His leading will we be able to walk in spiritual power.

GOD'S WORD FOR YOU

So get rid of all uncleanness and the rampant outgrowth of wickedness, and in a humble (gentle, modest) spirit receive and welcome the Word which implanted and rooted [in your hearts] contains the power to save your souls.

JAMES 1:21

For the Word that God speaks is alive and full of power [making it active, operative, energizing, and effective]; it is sharper than any two-edged sword, penetrating to the dividing line of the breath of life (soul) and [the immortal] spirit, and of joints and marrow [of the deepest parts of our nature], exposing and sifting and analyzing and judging the very thoughts and purposes of the heart.

HEBREWS 4:12

Power in the Word

Once a person is filled with the Holy Spirit, God is not finished with him. He is just beginning. The tool the Holy Spirit uses to powerfully bring about the transformation of our characters is the Word of God.

The devil's work in the believer's life is based upon deception, which results when lies are believed. As long as I believe the wrong thing, I remain deceived and powerless. When God's Word of truth uncovers those lies, the truth sets us free.

Only the Word of God has this power, and only God can change us. The Word exposes wrong motives, wrong thoughts, and wrong words. Truth can set us free from guilt, self-rejection, condemnation, self-hatred, the works of the flesh, and every lie that we have bought into and brought into our lives. God is out to save and free our entire soul from corruption.

A sword in the sheath is of no value. It must be wielded and appropriately used. The Word of God is the believer's sword, and we must learn to apply it daily, getting it down in our heart, and speaking it out our mouth. The believer who does that is a major threat to Satan and a powerhouse for God.

Love the Word, study the Word, learn the Word.

GOD'S WORD FOR YOU

*. . . let everyone who is godly pray—pray to You in a
time when You may be found; surely when the great waters
[of trial] overflow, they shall not reach [the spirit in] him.*

PSALM 32:6

*He who dwells in the secret place of the Most High
shall remain stable and fixed under the shadow of the
Almighty [Whose power no foe can withstand].*

PSALM 91:1

POWER IN PRAYER

It's simple: If you don't spend time with God, you are cutting yourself off from His power. David tells us that it is in the secret place of the presence of God that we are protected. When we spend time with the Lord in prayer and in His Word, we are in the secret place. It is a place of peace and security where we can give Him our cares and trust Him to take care of us.

We really need to understand the awesomeness of God's presence and what is available to us as believers. Why in the world would we not want to spend time with God? Even Jesus would get up early in the morning to be alone with God. He knew the value of being in the presence of God.

Just dedicate a portion of your time to spend with God. Try not to be legalistic about it, but do try to be as regular with it as you can. Take time to read the Bible and any other Christian books that minister to you. Talk to God. Sometimes you may want to listen to Christian music and worship; other times you may just want to sit there and enjoy the silence. Open up your heart and let His presence into your life.

Spending time in the secret place of His presence changes you from what you are to what only He can make you to be.

GOD'S WORD FOR YOU

[The Servant of God says] The Lord God has given Me the tongue of a disciple and of one who is taught, that I should know how to speak a word in season to him who is weary. He wakens Me morning by morning, He wakens My ear to hear as a disciple [as one who is taught].

ISAIAH 50:4

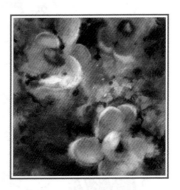

Power in Words

Words are awesome. Words are containers for power. God created the earth with His words (Hebrews 11:3). The Holy Spirit changes lives with words. People are encouraged or defeated because of words. Marriages break up because people don't say the right words.

Jesus said that His words are spirit, and they are life (John 6:63). But words can also speak death to you by speaking words that put a heaviness on you.

We need to learn to use our mouth for its God-intended purpose. He gave it to us to love people through our encouraging, positive, life-giving words. He gave it to us to give Him praise and thanks. Speaking the right word to a person at the right time can turn their whole life around. Words are powerful.

This is why knowing the Word of God is so important. We need to study it, learn it, and then speak it out according to our situations and needs. For instance, if you feel depressed, don't say, "I'm depressed." Take hold of the Word and say, "Why are you so downcast, O my soul? Put your hope in God." You will be absolutely amazed at how your life will change if you change the way you talk.

*Choose to be God's mouthpiece
and close the door to the devil.*

BEARING
SPIRITUAL
FRUIT

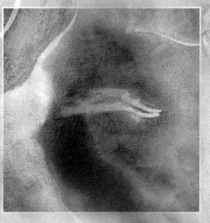

The great responsibility attached to Christianity is to walk in integrity—to "walk the walk," even when nobody notices.

GOD'S WORD FOR YOU

Beware of false prophets, who come to you dressed as sheep, but inside they are devouring wolves.

You will fully recognize them by their fruits. Do people pick grapes from thorns, or figs from thistles?

Even so, every healthy (sound) tree bears good fruit [worthy of admiration], but the sickly (decaying, worthless) tree bears bad (worthless) fruit.

A good (healthy) tree cannot bear bad (worthless) fruit, nor can a bad (diseased) tree bear excellent fruit [worthy of admiration].

Every tree that does not bear good fruit is cut down and cast into the fire.

Therefore, you will fully know them by their fruits.

MATTHEW 7:15–20

s i x

BEARING SPIRITUAL FRUIT

During my first few years of ministry, I spent a lot of my prayer time asking God for the special endowments of the gifts of the Holy Spirit to operate through me. To be a powerful minister, I certainly needed them. We all need them. But I didn't give much thought to the fruit of the Spirit. Then one day the Lord impressed upon me, "Joyce, if you would have put even one half as much energy and time into praying about and trying to develop the fruit of the Spirit as you have the gifts, you'd already have both."

As Christians, many of us pray that God will move powerfully through us to help others, and God wants us to pray this way. He has made available to us special endowments of supernatural energy that the Bible calls *spiritual gifts* to use for that very purpose. But I believe our first priority should be developing the fruit of the Spirit.

We are known by our fruit, not by our gifts. We are known to be Jesus' followers by our love for one another, and by our fruit Jesus is known. A display of the fruit of the Spirit, the nature of God, is a display of the character of Jesus Christ.

When people taste the fruit in us and see it is good, they want to find the Source of this fruit—this tree of life. We must show people that what we have is real before they will listen to what we say.

GOD'S WORD FOR YOU

But the fruit of the [Holy] Spirit [the work which His presence within accomplishes] is love, joy (gladness), peace, patience (an even temper, forbearance), kindness, goodness (benevolence), faithfulness,

Gentleness (meekness, humility), self-control (self-restraint, continence). Against such things there is no law [that can bring a charge].

GALATIANS 5:22–23

THE FRUIT OF THE SPIRIT

We are to go out into the world and let the Holy Spirit flow through us to show God's love—His joy, peace, patience, kindness, goodness, faithfulness, gentleness, and self-control—and help people with His gifts. By focusing on the importance God places on developing the fruit of His Spirit, we will find that a door for the release of our gifts will swing wide open.

When the Holy Spirit lives inside us, we have everything He has. His fruit is in us. The seed has been planted. We must allow the seed of the fruit to grow up and mature in us by cultivating it.

We can cultivate all the fruit by focusing on love and self-control, the first and last in the list. All of the fruit issue from love and actually are a form of love, but they are kept in place by self-control. If you are concentrating on developing the fruit of love, you won't become impatient or unkind with people. You will be good to them, supportive and faithful. Self-control helps us to make those little choices throughout the day to respond with the fruit, and soon we form a habit. If you continue to cultivate this habit, you will grow the fruit into an exceptional life in the Spirit.

When our fruit is "squeezed," and we get caught off guard, we discover how undeveloped our fruit is.

GOD'S WORD FOR YOU

Such hope never disappoints or deludes or shames us, for God's love has been poured out in our hearts through the Holy Spirit Who has been given to us.

ROMANS 5:5

And this I pray: that your love may abound yet more and more and extend to its fullest development in knowledge and all keen insight [that your love may display itself in greater depth of acquaintance and more comprehensive discernment] . . .

PHILIPPIANS 1:9

THE POWER OF LOVE

Even when we operate in the greater spiritual gifts, but without love, we are nothing but a big noise or someone who isn't doing anyone any good! Love is not theory or talk, but deeds. Love is actions, doing what needs to be done in every situation.

Concentrate on your love walk and examine your life—your attitudes, your thought life, what you say, how you treat people. How kind are you to people? What are you doing for people? How are you treating people who aren't treating you nicely? Our flesh may not always feel like loving others, but if we want to walk in spiritual power and defeat the enemy, we must say, "It is no longer I who live, but Christ the Messiah lives in me" (Galatians 2:20).

To abound in love is the most excellent thing we can do. And we must do everything with an excellent spirit. We cannot be an excellent person and not walk in love. How can we say that we are walking in love if we are not treating people excellently?

You have the Holy Spirit's power to do what is right—not just what you feel like doing.

Some people feel they need to blow their own horn with their gifts. They don't—they just need to learn to walk in love. The tree is known and judged by its fruit.

GOD'S WORD FOR YOU

*He who has no rule over his own spirit is like a city
that is broken down and without walls.*

PROVERBS 25:28

THE POWER OF SELF-CONTROL

In the world today, Christianity doesn't have a great reputation. The attitude people have about Christians can be painful sometimes because they see us from the world's perspective. But another part of it is, Christians often don't always live up to what they say they believe.

We will not operate in any of the fruit of the Spirit or walk in the power of God without self-control. The fruit of the Spirit is not about how we feel, but about what we choose to do. God gives us self-control so we can discipline ourselves. Without self-control, we cannot have the things we desire.

God wants to help us discipline our thoughts and our mouth. You may feel as though you don't have any discipline or control, but you do! If the Spirit of God lives in you, there it is. God has given us a spirit of power and of love and of a calm and well-balanced mind and discipline and self-control (2 Timothy 1:7).

In the presence of God we need the love of Christ to constrain us and grip our hearts. May all we do and say become an expression of the loving heart of God.

If feelings are your motto in life, then you can stamp disaster across your life. You will not experience victory and make decisions to do what you know you should do.

GOD'S WORD FOR YOU

So that the righteous and just requirement of the Law might be fully met in us who live and move not in the ways of the flesh but in the ways of the Spirit [our lives governed not by the standards and according to the dictates of the flesh, but controlled by the Holy Spirit].

For those who are according to the flesh and are controlled by its unholy desires set their minds on and pursue those things which gratify the flesh, but those who are according to the Spirit and are controlled by the desires of the Spirit set their minds on and seek those things which gratify the [Holy] Spirit.

ROMANS 8:4–5

WALK IN THE SPIRIT

Spiritual power comes with a price tag. In order to walk in the Spirit, we must say no to some things to which we would rather say yes, and yes to some things to which we would rather say no. We must follow the prompting of the Holy Spirit through our own spirit.

To walk in the Spirit requires that we stay filled with the Spirit. This is accomplished by continually choosing right thoughts, conversation, companionship, music, entertainment, etc.

To do God's will, we must be ready to suffer. If our flesh desires to walk one way and God's Spirit is leading us another way, a willful decision to be obedient will provoke suffering in the flesh.

The good news is, if we choose to walk in the Spirit daily, we will die to self-centeredness and gain freedom to serve God. We will experience righteousness, peace, and joy in the Holy Spirit. We will live in victory no matter what comes against us. That's living in power!

Invest in your future: Walk in the Spirit.
Start making right choices. Be persistent
and expect to be blessed.

GOD'S WORD FOR YOU

And do not grieve the Holy Spirit of God [do not offend or vex or sadden Him], by Whom you were sealed (marked, branded as God's own, secured) for the day of redemption (of final deliverance through Christ from evil and the consequences of sin).

EPHESIANS 4:30

Do Not Grieve the Spirit

I take a verse such as Ephesians 4:30 very seriously. I do not want to grieve the Holy Spirit, but how do I avoid doing it? Reading the verses surrounding it makes it clear that one thing that grieves the Holy Spirit is for people to mistreat one another. In verse 29 we are encouraged to edify others with the words of our mouth. Verse 31 exhorts us not to be bitter, angry, or contentious and to beware of slander, spite, and ill will. Then in verse 32 we are told to be kind to one another, forgiving readily and freely.

It comes back to our love walk and how the Holy Spirit has shed abroad the love of God in our hearts. It is He Who teaches us, convicting us of wrong conduct when we mistreat others. It is He Who works in us to give us a tender heart. Pray for such a heart.

When I realized that it grieved the Holy Spirit when I was sharp or hateful with someone, or when I stayed angry at someone, I began to take that kind of behavior more seriously. I also realized that what I was doing made me feel grieved as well. It made me feel sad or depressed, or I had a sense that something just wasn't right. All such disobedience is sin and grieves the Spirit, cutting off our spiritual power.

I have found the secret to being happy
all the time—it is to walk in love.

GOD'S WORD FOR YOU

Thank [God] in everything [no matter what the circumstances may be, be thankful and give thanks], for this is the will of God for you [who are] in Christ Jesus [the Revealer and Mediator of that will].

Do not quench (suppress or subdue) the [Holy] Spirit;

Do not spurn the gifts and utterances of the prophets [do not depreciate prophetic revelations nor despise inspired instruction or exhortation or warning].

But test and prove all things [until you can recognize] what is good; [to that] hold fast.

1 THESSALONIANS 5:18–21

Do Not Quench the Spirit

Paul tells us not to quench, suppress, or subdue the Holy Spirit. According to *Webster's*, *to quench* means to "put out," *to suppress* means "to check or stop (a natural flow)," and *to subdue* means "to make less intense." If we quench a fire, we put it out or extinguish it. We do not want to quench the Holy Spirit; instead, we want to make sure we do everything we can to increase His activity and flow in our life.

The previous verses in 1 Thessalonians give us rich insight into walking in spiritual power. From these Scriptures, it is clear that our attitude is very important. It is all about how we act, the behavior patterns we display. Our attitude involves our character, and our character begins with our thoughts.

It quenches the Spirit when we have a bad attitude such as bitterness, anger, unforgiveness, spitefulness, disrespect, vengefulness, a lack of appreciation, and the list goes on and on. The Holy Spirit flows through a godly attitude, not an ungodly one.

Regularly examine your heart and guard it with all diligence (Proverbs 4:23). It's your life source.

If we are smart enough not to swallow poison, we should also be intelligent enough not to allow Satan to poison our mind, attitude, and ultimately our life.

GOD'S WORD FOR YOU

That is why I would remind you to stir up (rekindle the embers of, fan the flame of, and keep burning) the [gracious] gift of God, [the inner fire] that is in you by means of the laying on of my hands [with those of the elders at your ordination].

For God did not give us a spirit of timidity (of cowardice, of craven and cringing and fawning fear), but [He has given us a spirit] of power and of love and of calm and well-balanced mind and discipline and self-control.

2 TIMOTHY 1:6–7

Keep Moving Forward

In our spiritual lives we are either aggressively going forward on purpose, or we are slipping backward. There is no such thing as dormant Christianity. We cannot put our Christian walk or spiritual power on hold. It is vital to keep pressing on. That is why Timothy was instructed to fan the flame and rekindle the fire that once burned in him.

Evidently, Timothy had taken a step backward, perhaps via fear. Anytime we get into fear, we begin to become immobile instead of active. Fear freezes us in place, so to speak; it prevents progress.

It is certainly easy to understand why Timothy may have lost his courage and confidence. It was a time of extreme persecution, and his mentor Paul was in jail. What if the same happened to him?

Yet Paul strongly encouraged Timothy to stir himself up, get back on track, remember the call on his life, resist fear, and remember that God had given him a spirit of power and of love and of a sound mind. All of this had come to him when he received the fullness of the Holy Spirit.

If we intend to stay stirred up in the Holy Spirit, we must choose our thoughts and words carefully.

GOD'S WORD FOR YOU

But I say, walk and live [habitually] in the [Holy] Spirit [responsive to and controlled and guided by the Spirit]; then you will certainly not gratify the cravings and desires of the flesh (of human nature without God).

GALATIANS 5:16

Always Be Led by the Spirit

Paul did not say the desires or the lusts of the flesh would die or no longer exist for the children of God. He said that we must choose to be led by the Holy Spirit, and by making that choice, we would not fulfill the lusts of the flesh that continually tempt us.

There are many things available to lead us—other people, the devil and his demons, the flesh (our own body, mind, will, or emotions), or the Holy Spirit. There are many voices in the world that are speaking to us, and often several at the same time.

It is imperative that we learn how to be led by the Holy Spirit. He alone knows the will of God and is sent to dwell in each of us to aid us in being all God has designed us to be and to have all God wants us to have. Being led by the Spirit means He leads us by peace and by wisdom, as well as by the Word of God. He speaks in a still, small voice in our heart or what we often call "the inward witness." Those who want to walk in spiritual power must learn to follow the inward witness and to respond quickly.

The Holy Spirit lives in each of us to help us!
We should lift up our entire life daily and say
with all our might, "Holy Spirit, You are
welcome to move in power in my life!"

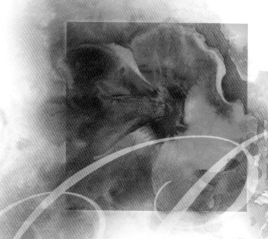

THE JOY OF
BELIEVING PRAYER

SIMPLE, BELIEVING PRAYER

*If we don't pray, the best
thing that can happen is
nothing, so that things will
stay the way they are,
which is frightening
enough in itself. We all
need change, and the way
to get it is through prayer.*

GOD'S WORD FOR YOU

And when you pray, do not heap up phrases (multiply words, repeating the same ones over and over) as the Gentiles do, for they think they will be heard for their much speaking. [I Kings 18:25-29.]

MATTHEW 6:7

one

SIMPLE,
BELIEVING PRAYER

or many years I was dissatisfied with my prayer life. I was committed to praying every morning, but I always felt something was missing. I finally asked God what was wrong, and He responded in my heart by saying, "Joyce, you don't feel that your prayers are good enough." I was not enjoying prayer because I had no confidence that my prayers were acceptable.

Too often we get caught up in our own works concerning prayer. Sometimes we try to pray so long, loud, or fancy that we lose sight of the fact that prayer is simply conversation with God. The length or loudness or eloquence of our prayer is not the issue. It is the sincerity of our heart and the confidence that God hears and will answer us that is important.

We must develop the confidence that even if we simply say, "God help me," He hears and will answer. We can depend on God to be faithful to do what we have asked Him to do as long as our request is in accordance with His will. We should know that He wants to help us because He is our Helper (Hebrews 13:6).

Simple, believing prayer comes straight
out of the heart and goes straight
to the heart of God.

GOD'S WORD FOR YOU

Two men went up into the temple [enclosure] to pray, the one a Pharisee and the other a tax collector.

The Pharisee took his stand ostentatiously and began to pray thus before and with himself: God, I thank You that I am not like the rest of men—extortioners (robbers), swindlers [unrighteous in heart and life], adulterers—or even like this tax collector here.

I fast twice a week; I give tithes of all that I gain.

But the tax collector, [merely] standing at a distance, would not even lift up his eyes to heaven, but kept striking his breast, saying, O God, be favorable (be gracious, be merciful) to me, the especially wicked sinner that I am!

I tell you, this man went down to his home justified (forgiven and made upright and in right standing with God), rather than the other man; for everyone who exalts himself will be humbled, but he who humbles himself will be exalted.

LUKE 18:10-14

Humble Prayer

For prayer to be sincere, it must come from a humble heart. In this lesson on prayer taught by Jesus Himself, we see that the Pharisee prayed "ostentatiously," meaning that he prayed pretentiously, making an extravagant outward show. There was nothing secret or even sincere about his prayer. It even says that he prayed "before and with himself." In other words, his prayers never got two inches away from himself; he was all caught up in what *he* was doing.

The second man in the story, a despised tax collector and a "wicked sinner" in most people's eyes, humbled himself, bowed his head, and quietly, with humility, asked God to help him. In response to his sincere, humble prayer, a lifetime of sin was wiped away in a moment. This is the power of simple, believing prayer.

Build your faith on the fact that humble, believing prayer is powerful. Believe that you can pray anywhere, anytime, about anything. Believe that your prayers don't have to be perfect or eloquent or long. Keep them simple and full of faith.

We receive the grace of God by humbling ourselves before Him, casting all our cares upon Him, and trusting Him to take care of them as He has promised in His Word.

GOD'S WORD FOR YOU

And I tell you, you are Peter [Greek, Petros—a large piece of rock], and on this rock [Greek, petra—a huge rock like Gibraltar] I will build My church, and the gates of Hades (the powers of the infernal region) shall not overpower it [or be strong to its detriment or hold out against it].

I will give you the keys of the kingdom of heaven; and whatever you bind (declare to be improper and unlawful) on earth must be what is already bound in heaven; and whatever you loose (declare lawful) on earth must be what is already loosed in heaven. [Isa. 22:22.]

MATTHEW 16:18-19

AUTHORITY THROUGH PRAYER

Since we are not only physical creatures but spiritual beings as well, we are able to stand in the physical realm and affect the spiritual realm. This is a very definite privilege and advantage. We can go into the spiritual realm through prayer and bring about action that will cause change in a situation. *God is a Spirit* . . . (John 4:24), and every answer we need to every situation is with Him.

Jesus told Peter that He would give him the keys of the Kingdom of heaven. Keys unlock doors, and I believe those keys (at least in part) can represent various types of prayer. Jesus went on to teach Peter about the power of binding and loosing, which operates on the same spiritual principle.

Jesus was also speaking to Peter about the power of faith in verse 18, and we know that one way faith is released is through prayer. The power of binding and loosing is also exercised in prayer.

When you and I pray about deliverance from some bondage in our lives or in the life of another, we are, in effect, binding that problem and loosing an answer. The act of prayer binds evil and looses good.

Jesus has conferred on us the power and authority to use the keys of the Kingdom to bring to pass the will of God on earth.

GOD'S WORD FOR YOU

Now Peter and John were going up to the temple at the hour of prayer. . . .

ACTS 3:1

THE HABIT OF PRAYER

Many people feel vaguely guilty about their prayer life because they compare themselves to others. God is a creative God and wants each person to have his or her own individual prayer life. It doesn't have to be just like that of anyone else.

Yes, there are definite principles of prayer that need to be followed. As we see here in the book of Acts, the early disciples set aside certain hours of the day when they would go to a designated place to pray. That is good self-discipline, but that should be the start of prayer and not the finish. We should discipline ourselves to establish a prayer schedule that is individually suited to us and then stick to it until it becomes such a part of our lifestyle that we do it without even thinking.

All day we can continue to communicate with the Lord, praising and worshiping Him, thanking Him for His presence with us and asking His help in all our problems. Then just before we go to sleep at night, we can offer up a final prayer of gratitude for the blessings of the day and a request for a peaceful and refreshing night's sleep.

God wants prayer to be a normal part of our lives.

GOD'S WORD FOR YOU

Be unceasing in prayer [praying perseveringly].

1 THESSALONIANS 5:17

Pray at all times (on every occasion, in every season) in the Spirit, with all [manner of] prayer and entreaty. To that end keep alert and watch with strong purpose and perseverance, interceding in behalf of all the saints (God's consecrated people).

EPHESIANS 6:18

PRAY WITHOUT CEASING

The *King James Version* of this verse says, "Pray without ceasing."

I used to wonder, *Lord, how can I ever get to the place that I am able to pray without ceasing?* To me the phrase "without ceasing" meant nonstop, without ever quitting. I couldn't see how that was possible.

Now I have a better understanding of what Paul was saying. He meant that prayer should be like breathing, something we do continually but often unconsciously. Our physical bodies require breathing. Likewise, our spiritual bodies are designed to be nurtured and sustained by continual prayer.

The problem is that because of religious thinking we have the mistaken idea that if we don't keep up a certain schedule of prayer we are missing the mark. If we become too "religious" about prayer, thinking we must do it one way or the other because that is how someone else does it, we will bring condemnation on ourselves. The important lesson about prayer is not the posture or the time or place but learning to pray in faith—at all times, unceasingly.

It is the Holy Spirit Who will lead you into prayer without ceasing.

143

GOD'S WORD FOR YOU

Do not fret or have any anxiety about anything, but in every circumstance and in everything, by prayer and petition (definite requests), with thanksgiving, continue to make your wants known to God.

And God's peace [shall be yours, that tranquil state of a soul assured of its salvation through Christ, and so fearing nothing from God and being content with its earthly lot of whatever sort that is, that peace] which transcends all understanding shall garrison and mount guard over your hearts and minds in Christ Jesus.

PHILIPPIANS 4:6-7

PRAYER PRODUCES PEACE

In this passage the apostle Paul does not say, "Pray and worry." Instead, he says, "Pray and don't worry." Why are we to pray and not worry? Because prayer is supposed to be the way we *cast our care* upon the Lord.

When the devil tries to give us care, we are supposed to turn and give that care to God. That's what prayer is, our acknowledgment to the Lord that we cannot carry our burden of care, so we lay it all on Him. If we pray about something and then keep on worrying about it, we are mixing a positive and a negative. The two cancel each other out so that we end up right back where we started—at zero.

Prayer is a positive force; worry is a negative force. The Lord has told me the reason many people operate at zero power level spiritually is that they cancel out their positive prayer power by giving in to the negative power of worry.

As long as we are worrying, we are not trusting God. It is only by trusting, by having faith and confidence in the Lord, that we are able to enter into His rest and enjoy the peace that transcends all understanding.

Make a decision now to cast all your care on the Lord and begin to watch Him take care of you.

GOD'S WORD FOR YOU

Come to Me, all you who labor and are heavy-laden and overburdened, and I will cause you to rest. [I will ease and relieve and refresh your souls.]

Take My yoke upon you and learn of Me, for I am gentle (meek) and humble (lowly) in heart, and you will find rest (relief and ease and refreshment and recreation and blessed quiet) for your souls.

MATTHEW 11:28-29

For we who have believed [adhered to and trusted in and relied on God) do enter that rest.

HEBREWS 4:3

PRAYER PRODUCES REST

If we are not at rest, we are not believing, because the fruit of believing is rest.

For many years of my life I would claim, "Oh, I'm believing God; I'm trusting the Lord." But I was not doing either of those things. I didn't know the first thing about believing God or trusting the Lord. I was anxious, panicky, irritable, and on edge all the time.

Just as we can be involved in outward activity, we can be involved in inward activity. God wants us not only to enter into His rest in our body, He also wants us to enter into His rest in our soul.

To me, finding rest, relief, ease, refreshment, recreation, and blessed quiet for my soul means finding freedom from mental activity. It means not having to live in the torment of reasoning, always trying to come up with an answer I don't have. I don't have to worry; instead, I can remain in a place of quiet peace and rest through prayer.

If we are truly believing God and trusting the Lord, we have entered into His rest. We have prayed and cast our care upon Him and are now abiding in the perfect peace of His holy presence.

You can speak His Word to your raging soul and tortured mind just as Jesus spoke to the wind and waves and said, "Peace, be still."

GOD'S WORD FOR YOU

Through Him also we have [our] access (entrance, introduction) by faith into this grace (state of God's favor) in which we [firmly and safely] stand. And let us rejoice and exult in our hope of experiencing and enjoying the glory of God.

Moreover [let us also be full of joy now!] let us exult and triumph in our troubles and rejoice in our sufferings, knowing that pressure and affliction and hardship produce patient and unswerving endurance.

And endurance (fortitude) develops maturity of character (approved faith and tried integrity). And character [of this sort] produces [the habit of] joyful and confident hope.

ROMANS 5:2-4

PRAYER PRODUCES PATIENCE AND HOPE

It is easy to say, "Don't worry." But to actually do that requires experience with God. I don't think there is any way a person can fully overcome the habit of worry, anxiety, and fear and develop the habit of peace, rest, and hope without years of experience.

That's why it is so important to continue to have faith and trust in God in the very midst of trials and tribulations. We must steadfastly resist the temptation to give up and quit when the going gets rough—and keeps on getting rougher over a long period of time. It is in those hard, trying times that the Lord is building in us the patience, endurance, and character that will eventually produce the habit of joyful and confident hope.

When you and I are in the midst of battle against our spiritual enemy, every round we go through produces valuable experience and strength. Each time we endure an attack, we become stronger. If we hang in there and refuse to give up, sooner or later we will be more than the devil can handle. When that happens, we will have reached spiritual maturity.

*We serve a God Who is so marvelous
that He can work out things for our good
that Satan intends for our harm.*

GOD'S WORD FOR YOU

All of these with their minds in full agreement devoted themselves steadfastly to prayer.

ACTS 1:14

United or Corporate Prayer

Whenever believers are united in corporate prayer, there is great power present. Jesus Himself said, "For wherever two or three are gathered (drawn together as My followers) in (into) My name, there I AM in the midst of them" (Matthew 18:20).

Throughout the book of Acts we read that the people of God came together "with one accord" (Acts 2:1, 46; 4:24; 5:12; 15:25 KJV). And it was their united faith, their corporate agreement, and the presence of Jesus by the power of the Holy Spirit that made their prayers so effective. They saw God move in mighty ways to confirm the truth of His Word as they gave testimony to their faith in Jesus.

Then in Philippians 2:2 we are told by the apostle Paul, "Fill up and complete my joy by living in harmony and being of the same mind and one in purpose, having the same love, being in full accord and of one harmonious mind and intention."

Paul is giving us an important principle about corporate prayer. If we will heed these words and come into harmony and agreement with one another and with God, we will experience the same kind of powerful results the first-century disciples enjoyed in the book of Acts.

When you come together to pray,
expect God to show His power!

GOD'S WORD FOR YOU

And the Lord said to Moses, I have seen this people, and behold, it is a stiff-necked people;

Now therefore let Me alone, that My wrath may burn hot against them and that I may destroy them; but I will make of you a great nation.

But Moses besought the Lord his God, and said, Lord, why does Your wrath blaze hot against Your people, whom You have brought forth out of the land of Egypt with great power and a mighty hand?

[Earnestly] remember Abraham, Isaac, and Israel, Your servants, to whom You swore by Your own self and said to them, I will multiply your seed as the stars of the heavens, and all this land that I have spoken of will I give to your seed, and they shall inherit it forever.

Then the Lord turned from the evil which He had thought to do to His people.

EXODUS 32:9-11, 13-14

GOD CHANGES PEOPLE THROUGH PRAYER

Moses' intercession for the children of Israel is a stirring example that depicts how sincere prayer can change God's mind.

There are times when I can sense that God is getting weary of putting up with someone who is not obeying Him, and I will find myself being led to pray for God to be merciful to that person and to give that individual another chance.

As Jesus told His disciples at Gethsemane, we should "watch and pray" (Matthew 26:41 KJV). We need to pray for one another, not judge and criticize each other. If we watch people, we can see when they need encouragement, when they are depressed, fearful, insecure, or experiencing any number of obvious problems. God allows us to discern their need in order to be part of the answer, not part of the problem. Remember we are not the potter. God is, and we certainly don't know how to "fix" people.

People who are hurting don't need someone with a spirit of pride trying to *fix* them; they need acceptance, love, and prayer.

Pray! Pray! Pray! It is the only way to get things accomplished in God's economy. If we do things His way, we always get good results.

We need to do the praying and let God do the working.

GOD'S WORD FOR YOU

For we are fellow workmen (joint promoters, laborers together) with and for God; you are God's garden and vineyard and field under cultivation, [you are] God's building.

1 CORINTHIANS 3:9

Do you not discern and understand that you [the whole church at Corinth] are God's temple (His sanctuary), and that God's Spirit has His permanent dwelling in you [to be at home in you, collectively as a church and also individually]?

1 CORINTHIANS 3:16

WE ARE THE PLACE OF PRAYER

Under the Old Covenant, the temple was the house of God, the place of prayer for His people, the children of Israel. And no expense was spared to beautify the temple where the people came to worship the Lord their God. In 1 Kings 6 we have a description of Solomon's temple, which contained the ark of the covenant, God's pledge of His presence.

Under the New Covenant the apostle Paul instructs us that God's presence is now a mystery revealed of Christ in us, "the Hope of glory" (Colossians 1:27). Because of the union we now have in Christ, we are God's living temple. We are indwelt by the Holy Spirit, a building still under construction, but nonetheless His house, His tabernacle. That is why Paul goes to great length to tell us to live a holy life. We are a temple of the living God.

Whereas the children of Israel had to go to a specific place to offer their worship with detailed instructions, we have the incredible privilege of worshiping God anywhere and at any time. Therefore, we should be called a house of prayer.

We become the sanctuary of God because of the presence of the Holy One in us.

HOW TO PRAY EFFECTIVELY

*There is nothing more powerful
to change our lives and
the lives of those around us
than God's hand moving in response
to our heartfelt, continued prayer.*

GOD'S WORD FOR YOU

*The earnest (heartfelt, continued) prayer of a
righteous man makes tremendous power available
[dynamic in its working].*

JAMES 5:16

t w o

HOW TO PRAY
EFFECTIVELY

 reached a point in my prayer life where I felt frustrated, so I began to seek God about it. I wanted the assurance that "the earnest, heartfelt prayer of a righteous man makes tremendous power available, dynamic in its working." I wanted God's power made available to change that situation or bless that person's life over which I was praying.

If we're going to learn how to pray effectively, we have to say, "Lord, teach me to pray." He will show you the keys to praying more effectively. Keys lock and unlock. Keys reflect authority. Whoever has the keys has the authority. When we pray this way, we're asking the Lord to reveal His prayer principles that will make our prayers effective.

I encourage you to start seeking God's will when you pray, because there will be an anointing on prayer that is in line with His will. God showed me that to pray fervently means to put your whole self, all of your attention, your mind, your will, your emotions, all of you into what you're praying about. He is more concerned with the quality of prayer than the quantity of prayer.

Be shamelessly persistent in prayer.

GOD'S WORD FOR YOU

The effective, fervent prayer of a righteous man avails much.

JAMES 5:16 NKJV

The heartfelt supplication of a righteous man exerts a mighty influence.

JAMES 5:16 WEYMOUTH

. . . The prayers of the righteous have a powerful effect.

JAMES 5:16 MOFFATT

FERVENT PRAYER

For prayer to be effective it must be fervent. However, if we misunderstand the word *fervent*, we may feel that we have to "work up" some strong emotion before we pray; otherwise, our prayers will not be effective.

I know there were many years when I believed this way, and perhaps you have been likewise confused or deceived. Look at some of the other translations of this verse that may make its meaning clearer: "fervent prayer . . . avails much"; "exerts a mighty influence"; "have a powerful effect."

I believe this scripture means that our prayers must come out of our heart and not just our head.

At times I experience a great deal of emotion while at prayer. Sometimes I even cry. But there are plenty of times when I don't feel emotional. Believing prayer is not possible if we base the value of our prayers on feelings. I remember enjoying so much those prayer times when I could *feel* God's presence, and then wondering what was wrong during the times when I didn't *feel* anything. I learned after a while that faith is not based on *feelings* in the emotions but on knowledge in the heart.

❧

*Trust that your earnest, heartfelt prayers
are effectual because your faith is in Him, not in
your own ability to live holy or pray eloquently.*

GOD'S WORD FOR YOU

. . . The effective, fervent prayer of a righteous man avails much.

Elijah was a man with a nature like ours, and he prayed earnestly that it would not rain; and it did not rain on the land for three years and six months.

JAMES 5:16-17

THE PRAYERS OF A RIGHTEOUS MAN

James tells us that the fervent prayer of a "righteous" man is powerful. This means a man who is not under condemnation—one who has confidence in God and in the power of prayer. It does not mean a man without any imperfection in his life.

Elijah was a man of God who did not always behave perfectly, but he did not allow his imperfections to steal his confidence in God. Elijah had faith, but he also had fear. He was obedient, but at times he was also disobedient. He loved God and wanted to fulfill His will and calling upon his life. But sometimes he gave in to human weaknesses and tried to avoid the consequences of that will and calling.

In 1 Kings 18 we see him moving in tremendous power, calling down fire from heaven and slaying 450 prophets of Baal. Then immediately we see him fearfully running from Jezebel, becoming negative and depressed, and even wanting to die.

Like many of us, Elijah let his emotions get the upper hand. He was a human being just like us, and yet he prayed powerful prayers. His example should give us enough "scriptural power" to defeat condemnation when it rises up to tell us we cannot pray powerfully because of our weaknesses and faults.

*Never underestimate the power
of effective, fervent prayer!*

GOD'S WORD FOR YOU

And when you pray, do not keep on babbling like pagans, for they think they will be heard because of their many words. Do not be like them, for your Father knows what you need before you ask him.

MATTHEW 6:7-8 NIV

*S*HORT AND SIMPLE

I believe God has instructed me to pray and make my requests with as few words as possible. If I can keep my request very simple and not confuse the issue by trying to come up with too many words, my prayer actually seems to be more clear and powerful.

We need to spend our energy releasing our faith, not repeating phrases over and over that only serve to make the prayer long and involved.

It has actually been difficult for me to keep my prayers short and simple. I began to realize that my problem in praying was that I didn't have faith that my prayer would get through if it was short, simple, and to the point. I had fallen into the same trap that many people do—"the-longer-the-better" mentality. I don't mean that I am advocating praying only for a short period of time, but I am suggesting that each prayer be simple, direct, to the point, and filled with faith.

Now as I follow God's direction to keep it simple and make my request with the least amount of words possible, I experience a much greater release of my faith, and I know that God has heard me and will answer.

If your prayers are complicated, simplify them.
If you are not praying enough, pray more.

GOD'S WORD FOR YOU

Keep on asking and it will be given you; keep on seeking and you will find; keep on knocking [reverently] and [the door] will be opened to you.

For everyone who keeps on asking receives; and he who keeps on seeking finds; and to him who keeps on knocking, [the door] will be opened.

MATTHEW 7:7-8

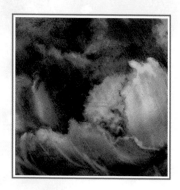

How Many Times Should I Pray?

I don't believe we can make any strict rules on the subject of how often to pray about the same thing. I do think there are some guidelines that may apply to help us have even more confidence in the power of prayer.

If my children need something, I would want them to trust me to do what they asked me to do. I wouldn't mind, and might even like it, if they occasionally said, "Boy, Mom, I'm sure looking forward to those new shoes." That statement would declare to me that they believed I was going to do what I promised. They would actually be reminding me of my promise, but in a way that would not question my integrity.

I believe sometimes when we ask God the same thing over and over, it is a sign of doubt and unbelief, not of faith and persistence.

When I ask the Lord for something in prayer, and that request comes to my mind later, I talk to Him about it again. But when I do, I refrain from asking Him the same thing as if I think He didn't hear me the first time. I thank the Lord that He is working on the situation I prayed about previously.

*Faithful, persistent prayer builds even more faith
and confidence in us as we continue to pray.*

GOD'S WORD FOR YOU

And this is the confidence (the assurance, the privilege of boldness) which we have in Him: [we are sure] that if we ask anything (make any request) according to His will (in agreement with His own plan), He listens to and hears us.

And if (since) we [positively] know that He listens to us in whatever we ask, we also know [with settled and absolute knowledge] that we have [granted us as our present possessions] the requests made of Him.

1 JOHN 5:14-15

BELIEVE GOD HEARS YOU!

When you pray, believe God hears you!

In John 11:41-42, just before Jesus called Lazarus forth from the tomb, Jesus prayed: "Father, I thank You that You have heard Me. Yes, I know You always hear and listen to Me, but I have said this on account of and for the benefit of the people standing around, so that they may believe that You did send Me [that You have made Me Your Messenger]." What confidence!

Satan does not want us to have that kind of confidence either. But I encourage you one more time: *Be confident!* Make a decision that you are a believer, not a beggar. Go to the throne in Jesus' name—His name will get attention!

Because my ministry is broadcast on TV, a few people know who I am, and some people like to use my name. My employees like to say, "I work for Joyce Meyer," and my children like to say, "Joyce Meyer is my mother." They think those they are approaching may give them more favor if they mention my name.

If that works for us as human beings, just think how well it must work in the heavenly realm—especially when we use the name that is above all other names—the blessed name of Jesus! (Philippians 2:9-11).

❦

Go to God in prayer—boldly. With confidence.
In the name of Jesus.

GOD'S WORD FOR YOU

Then He was praying in a certain place; and when He stopped, one of His disciples said to Him, Lord, teach us to pray, [just] as John taught his disciples.

And He said to them, When you pray, say: Our Father Who is in heaven, hallowed be Your name, Your kingdom come. Your will be done [held holy and revered] on earth as it is in heaven.

Give us daily our bread [food for the morrow].

And forgive us our sins, for we ourselves also forgive everyone who is indebted to us [who has offended us or done us wrong]. And bring us not into temptation but rescue us from evil.

LUKE 11:1-4

KNOW GOD AS YOUR FATHER

For many years I prayed the "Lord's Prayer," and I no more knew God as my Father than anything! I didn't have any kind of a close personal relationship with God. I was just repeating something I had learned.

If you want to be effective in your prayer life, you need to know God as your Father. When the disciples asked Jesus to teach them to pray, He taught them what we call the "Lord's Prayer," which is a spiritual treasure house of principles for prayer. But foremost, Jesus started out by instructing them to say, "Our Father Who is in heaven, hallowed be Your name."

Jesus was showing them the importance of seeing the privileged relationship He came to bring to every believer. He told them they needed to have a relationship with God as their Father if they expected to go to Him in prayer. Don't go to God as some ogre that you're afraid of, but develop a Father-child relationship with Him. That intimate relationship will give you liberty to ask Him for things you would not have asked for if you had a starchy, stiff relationship with Him.

Our heavenly Father longs to give good gifts to His children.

❧

When you pray, remember you have a loving Father Who is listening.

GOD'S WORD FOR YOU

And He said to them, Which of you who has a friend
will go to him at midnight and will say to him, Friend,
lend me three loaves [of bread],

For a friend of mine who is on a journey has just
come, and I have nothing to put before him;

And he from within will answer, Do not disturb me;
the door is now closed, and my children are with me in the
bed; I cannot get up and supply you [with anything]?

I tell you, although he will not get up and supply him
anything because he is his friend, yet because of his
shameless persistence and insistence he will get up and give
him as much as he needs.

LUKE 11:5-8

Become a Friend of God

The key to this scripture is *friendship*. The man in the story went at midnight to get bread for his friend in need. If the person you're going to isn't your friend, you will not shamelessly persist. Jesus was telling His disciples that God is much more willing to give us what we need than the man in the parable was to give to his friend.

Jesus said, "You are My friends if you keep on doing the things which I command you to do" (John 15:14). We're talking about a right heart attitude, that you're going to obey God no matter what it costs you. That's one of the criteria for being a friend of God. You also become His friend because you spend a lot of time with Him.

Isaiah 41:8 says, "But you, Israel, My servant, Jacob, whom I have chosen, the offspring of Abraham My friend." What an awesome thing to have God call you His friend. When God was going to bring judgment, He said, "Shall I hide from Abraham [My friend and servant] what I am going to do. . . ?" (Genesis 18:7). And as His friend, you can expect to have firsthand knowledge about what God is doing.

The closer friend you become with God,
the more boldness you have when you pray.

GOD'S WORD FOR YOU

Let us then fearlessly and confidently and boldly draw near to the throne of grace (the throne of God's unmerited favor to us sinners), that we may receive mercy [for our failures] and find grace to help in good time for every need [appropriate help and well-timed help, coming just when we need it].

HEBREWS 4:16

BE BOLD!

When you and I pray, we need to make sure we approach God as believers, not as beggars. Remember, according to Hebrews 4:16, we are to come boldly to the throne: not beggarly, but boldly; not belligerently, but boldly.

Be sure to keep the balance. Stay respectful, but be bold. Approach God with confidence. Believe He delights in your prayers and is ready to answer any request that is in accordance with His will.

As believers, we should know the Word of God, which is His will; therefore, it should be easy for us to pray according to God's will. Don't approach God wondering if what you are asking is His will. Settle that issue in your heart *before* you pray.

As you and I come boldly before the throne of God's grace, covered with the blood of Jesus, asking in faith according to His Word and in the name of His Son Jesus Christ, we can know that we have the petitions that we ask of Him. Not because we are perfect or worthy of ourselves, or because God owes us anything, but because He loves us and wants to give us what we need to do the job He has called us to do.

Jesus has purchased a glorious inheritance for us by the shedding of His blood. As joint-heirs with Him, we can pray boldly.

GOD'S WORD FOR YOU

But you, beloved, build yourselves up [founded] on your most holy faith [make progress, rise like an edifice higher and higher], praying in the Holy Spirit.

JUDE 20

PRAY IN THE SPIRIT

Just as Ephesians 6:18 tells us that we are not only to pray at all times with all manner of prayers, we are also told here by Jude that our prayers are to be "in the Holy Spirit." The apostle Paul tells us in Romans 8:26 that when we don't know how to pray, the Holy Spirit knows how to pray in our weakness.

It is the Holy Spirit of God within us Who provokes us and leads us to pray. Rather than delaying, we need to learn to yield to the leading of the Spirit as soon as we sense it. That is part of learning to pray all manner of prayers at all times, wherever we may be, and whatever we may be doing.

Our motto should be that of the old spiritual song, "Every time I feel the Spirit moving in my heart, I will pray." If we know we can pray anytime and anywhere, we won't feel we have to wait until just the right moment or place to pray.

When we are praying in the Holy Spirit, we can know that our prayers are reaching the throne of God and will be answered.

Ask the Holy Spirit to get involved in everything you do. He is the Helper, and He is waiting for you to ask.

GOD'S WORD FOR YOU

For God did not give us a spirit of timidity (of cowardice, of craven and cringing and fawning fear), but [He has given us a spirit] of power and of love and of calm and well-balanced mind and discipline and self-control.

2 TIMOTHY 1:7

PRAY AND FEAR NOT

God wants us to pray about everything and fear nothing. We could avoid a lot of problems if we would pray more, worry less, and fear less. Timothy says that God has not given us a spirit of fear. So when we feel fear, it is not from God. Any kind of fear—little fear, big fear—is not from God. It's from the devil. And the devil will try to intimidate us with all kinds of fear so that we do not pray.

If Abraham or Joshua or David had bowed their knee to fear when the task before them seemed overwhelming, they never would have experienced God as their abundant provision.

Prayer and God's Word will give you power to overcome fear. Memorize scriptures so when you feel fear, you can open your mouth and confess those scriptures out loud in faith-filled prayer. In fact, I think one of the most important things that we can do in our prayer time is walk around and confess the Word.

So often when we have something that we've got to confront and deal with, we start to dread and fear and wonder and reason what to do. Fear must be confronted. You can't wish fear away. You have to confront it with the Word of God.

❦

Put on the armor of God through prayer and stand against all the enemy's fiery darts of fear.

THE TYPES
OF PRAYER

*As believers we have spiritual
authority to do God's will
on earth through prayer.*

GOD'S WORD FOR YOU

First of all, then, I admonish and urge that petitions, prayers, intercessions, and thanksgivings be offered on behalf of all men,

For kings and all who are in positions of authority or high responsibility, that [outwardly] we may pass a quiet and undisturbed life [and inwardly] a peaceable one in all godliness and reverence and seriousness in every way.

For such [praying] is good and right, and [it is] pleasing and acceptable to God our Savior.

1 TIMOTHY 2:1-3

three

THE TYPES OF PRAYER

G od had to teach me some lessons about praying in faith, about understanding that the Holy Spirit was helping me in prayer, and that Jesus was interceding along with me (Romans 8:26; Hebrews 7:25). Two of the Persons of the Godhead are helping me pray!

How often are we to pray? At all times. How are we to pray? In the Spirit, with different kinds of prayer. I believe if we will allow Him to do so, the Holy Spirit will lead us into prayer without ceasing so it becomes like breathing. When that happens we can be continually offering up prayers.

Now I would like to discuss the types of prayer we see in the Word of God. We should be exercising all the various types of prayer on a regular basis. They are simple, can be prayed anywhere at any time, and are most effective when prayed from a believing heart.

God does hear our prayers and does respond to them. That is what makes them so powerful and so effective.

GOD'S WORD FOR YOU

Again I tell you, if two of you on earth agree (harmonize together, make a symphony together) about whatever [anything and everything] they may ask, it will come to pass and be done for them by My Father in heaven.

MATTHEW 18:19

THE PRAYER OF AGREEMENT

First, let me say that I believe this prayer can only be prayed by two or more people who are committed to living in agreement. This prayer is not for people who generally live in strife and then decide they need to agree for some type of miracle because they are desperate. God honors the prayers of those who pay the price to live in unity.

Because our prayer power multiplies when we are in agreement with those around us (1 Peter 3:7), we need to be in agreement all the time, not just when we face a crisis situation. There will be times in our life when what we are up against is something that is bigger than we are by ourselves. At such times, we will be wise to pray together with someone who is in agreement with us in that situation.

If you feel you have nobody in your life with whom you can agree in prayer, don't despair. You and the Holy Spirit can agree. He is here on the earth with you and in you as a child of God.

There is power in agreement! Pray the prayer of agreement, especially when you feel the need for a little extra prayer power!

GOD'S WORD FOR YOU

Hear my prayer, O Lord, give ear to my supplications! Answer me in Your faithfulness, in Your righteousness!

PSALM 143:1 NASB

Oh, that I might have my request, and that God would grant me the thing that I long for!

JOB 6:8

THE PRAYER OF PETITION

This prayer is by far the most often used. When we petition God, we ask for something for ourselves. Another word for petition is *requisition*. It is a demand or request made on something to which a person is legally entitled but not yet in possession of, as in the military when an officer requisitions equipment or supplies for his men. As an officer of the United States Army, he is entitled to that material, but in order to receive it he has to submit a definite request for it.

When we come to the Lord with a petition, we are requisitioning from Him what He has already set aside to provide for us when the need arises. For that reason, we frequently exercise our right to petition God. It is, of course, not wrong to ask God to do things for us, but our petitions should be well-balanced with praise and thanksgiving.

We can be bold in petitioning God for any type of need in our lives. We are not restricted to a certain number of requests per day. We can feel at ease talking to God about anything that concerns us, for He already knows what we need and is willing to grant us our petitions (Matthew 6:8).

When you are in trouble, go to the Throne before you go to the phone.

GOD'S WORD FOR YOU

Speak out to one another in psalms and hymns and spiritual songs, offering praise with voices [and instruments] and making melody with all your heart to the Lord,

At all times and for everything giving thanks in the name of our Lord Jesus Christ to God the Father.

EPHESIANS 5:19-20

Through Him, therefore, let us constantly and at all times offer up to God a sacrifice of praise, which is the fruit of lips that thankfully acknowledge and confess and glorify His name. [Lev. 7:12; Isa. 57:19; Hos. 14:2.]

HEBREWS 13:15

THE PRAYER OF PRAISE AND WORSHIP

Praise is a narration or a tale in which we recount the good qualities about an individual, in this case, God. We should praise the Lord continually. By continually, I mean all throughout the day. We should praise Him for His mighty works, the wonders He has created, and even the works of grace He is yet to do in each of our lives.

A sacrifice of praise means doing it even when we don't feel like it. We should praise God for His goodness, mercy, loving-kindness, grace, long-suffering, and patient nature in the hard times as well as the good. While we are waiting to see the fulfillment of our prayers, we are to be continually offering up to God the fruit of lips that thankfully acknowledge and confess and glorify His name.

It is not our responsibility to worry and fret or try to play God by taking into our own hands situations that should be left to Him alone. Instead, it is our responsibility to cast our care upon the Lord, trusting Him, praying without worry, avoiding works of the flesh, continuing in obedience, bearing good fruit, and offering Him the sacrifice of praise.

May a sacrifice of praise continually be in our mouths for the marvelous works of grace He has done for us.

GOD'S WORD FOR YOU

Thank [God] in everything [no matter what the circumstances may be, be thankful and give thanks], for this is the will of God for you [who are] in Christ Jesus [the Revealer and Mediator of that will].

1 THESSALONIANS 5:18

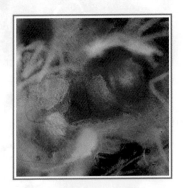

THE PRAYER OF THANKSGIVING

After telling us to pray without ceasing, the apostle Paul directs us to give thanks to God in everything, no matter what our circumstances may be, stating that this is the will of God for us.

Just as prayer is to be a lifestyle for us, so thanksgiving is to be a lifestyle for us. Giving thanks to God should not be something we do once a day as we sit down somewhere and try to think of all the good things He has done for us and merely say, "Thanks, Lord."

That is empty religion, something we do simply because we think God requires it. True thanksgiving flows continually out of a heart that is full of gratitude and praise to God for Who He is as much as for what He does. It is not something that is done to meet a requirement, win favor, gain a victory, or qualify for a blessing.

The type of thanksgiving that God the Father desires is that which is provoked by the presence of His Holy Spirit within us Who moves upon us to express to the Lord verbally what we are feeling and experiencing spiritually.

We are to be thankful to God always, continually acknowledging, confessing, and glorifying His name in prayerful praise and worship.

GOD'S WORD FOR YOU

And I sought a man among them who should build up the wall and stand in the gap before Me for the land, that I should not destroy it, but I found none.

EZEKIEL 22:30

Therefore He is able also to save to the uttermost (completely, perfectly, finally, and for all time and eternity) those who come to God through Him, since He is always living to make petition to God and intercede with Him and intervene for them.

HEBREWS 7:25

THE PRAYER OF INTERCESSION

To intercede means to *stand in the gap* for someone else, to plead his case before the throne of God. If there is a breach in people's relationship with God due to a particular sin in their life, we have the privilege of placing ourselves in that breach and praying for them. We can intercede for them and expect to see them comforted and encouraged while they wait. We can also expect a timely breakthrough for them concerning their need being met.

I don't know what I would do if people did not intercede for me. I petition God to give me people to intercede for me and for the fulfillment of the ministry to which He has called me. We need each other's prayers of intercession.

Praying for others is equivalent to sowing seed. We must sow seed if we are to reap a harvest (Galatians 6:7). Sowing seed into the lives of other people through intercession is one sure way to reap a harvest in our own life. Each time we pray for someone else, we are inviting God to not only work in that person's life but also in our own.

Intercession is one of the most important ways we carry on the ministry of Jesus Christ that He began in this earth.

We can release God's power in the lives
of others by praying for them.

GOD'S WORD FOR YOU

Commit your way to the Lord [roll and repose each care of your load on Him]; trust (lean on, rely on, and be confident) also in Him and He will bring it to pass.

PSALM 37:5

Casting the whole of your care [all your anxieties, all your worries, all your concerns, once and for all] on Him, for He cares for you affectionately and cares about you watchfully.

1 PETER 5:7

THE PRAYER OF COMMITMENT

When we are tempted to worry or take the care of some situation in life, we should pray the prayer of commitment. God intervenes in our situations when we commit them to Him.

In my own life I found that the more I tried to take care of things myself, the bigger mess my life became. I was quite independent and found it difficult to humble myself and admit that I needed help. However, when I finally submitted to God in these areas and found the joy of casting all my care on Him, I could not believe I had lived so long under such huge amounts of pressure.

Commit to the Lord your children, your marriage, your personal relationships, and especially anything you may be tempted to be concerned about. In order to succeed at being ourselves, we must continually be committing ourselves to God, giving to Him those things that appear to be holding us back. Only God really knows what needs to be done, and He is the *only* One Who is qualified to do it. The more we sincerely commit ourselves to Him, the more progress we make.

A believer who can trust the Father when things do not seem to make sense is a mature believer.

GOD'S WORD FOR YOU

I appeal to you therefore, brethren, and beg of you in view of [all] the mercies of God, to make a decisive dedication of your bodies [presenting all your members and faculties] as a living sacrifice, holy (devoted, consecrated) and well pleasing to God, which is your reasonable (rational, intelligent) service and spiritual worship.

ROMANS 12:1

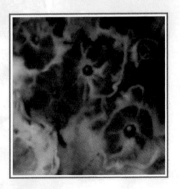

THE PRAYER OF CONSECRATION

Another life-changing type of prayer is the prayer of consecration, the prayer in which we give ourselves to God. In the prayer of consecration, we dedicate our lives and all that we are to Him.

In order for God to use us, we must give ourselves totally to Him. When we truly consecrate ourselves to the Lord, we relinquish the burden of trying to run our own lives. Consecration is a powerful act, but it must be sincere. It is quite easy to sing along with everyone else a song such as "I Surrender All." We may even feel moved emotionally, but the real test is found in daily life when circumstances don't always go the way we thought they would. Then we must sing again, "I Surrender All," consecrating ourselves to God afresh.

Consecration to God is the most important aspect of succeeding at being ourselves. We don't even know what we are supposed to be, let alone know how to become whatever it is. But as we regularly keep our lives on the altar in consecration to God, He will do the work that needs to be done in us so that He may do the work He desires to do *through* us.

When we consecrate ourselves to God,
He makes us into vessels fit for the Master's use.

GOD'S WORD FOR YOU

. . . the Lord is in His holy temple; let all the earth hush and keep silence before Him.

HABAKKUK 2:20

Our inner selves wait [earnestly] for the Lord; He is our Help and our Shield.

PSALM 33:20

THE PRAYER OF SILENCE

I also call this kind of prayer "waiting on the Lord." In our instant and fast-paced society, this spiritual discipline is often lacking. We want it and we want it right now! If we are always in such a hurry, we will miss out on the wisdom God wants to speak to our hearts if we will only be silent before Him.

Elijah was a man who learned the secret of silent, waiting prayer in His presence. After slaying the prophets of Baal, Elijah learned a valuable lesson on waiting on God. The Lord told Elijah to go stand on a mount and wait. A great wind came; then came a great earthquake and a great fire, but the Lord was in none of those. "After the fire [a sound of gentle stillness and] a still, small voice" (1 Kings 19:12).

David also learned to wait in the house of the Lord and "to meditate, consider, and inquire in His temple" (Psalm 27:4). If we want to learn how to pray effectively, then we are going to have to learn to sit in silence and listen for His Word. Waiting and listening takes our focus off of us and places it on Him, Who is the answer to all our needs.

It is often in silence when the power of God is moving the most mightily. Allow the Holy Spirit to teach you how to wait in His presence.

GOD'S WORD FOR YOU

Now when Jesus went into the region of Caesarea Philippi, He asked His disciples, Who do people say that the Son of Man is?

Simon Peter replied, You are the Christ, the Son of the loving God.

MATTHEW 16:13, 16

THE PRAYER OF CONFESSION

When Peter made that statement about Jesus being the Christ, the Son of the living God, he was releasing with his mouth the faith that was in his heart. The praying and confession of what we know in our hearts, revealed by the Holy Spirit, is a powerful way to pray and strengthen our faith.

We must understand that we establish the faith that is in our heart by the words we speak from our mouth, as the apostle Paul tells us in Romans 10:10: ". . . and with the mouth he confesses (declares openly and speaks out freely his faith) and confirms [his] salvation."

That is why prayer is so important. Because we establish the things we believe inwardly when we start talking about them outwardly. That is why confessing the Scriptures in prayer is also very powerful. When we do that, we are establishing things in the spiritual realm by the words we are speaking in the physical realm. And eventually what is established spiritually will be manifested physically.

You and I should be constantly confessing the Word of God, believing in our heart and confessing with our mouth what God has said about us in His Word.

We release heaven's power when we confess in the physical realm what God has already done for us in the spiritual realm

GOD'S WORD FOR YOU

Rejoice in the Lord always [delight, gladden yourselves in Him]; again I say, Rejoice!

PHILIPPIANS 4:4

I will rejoice in You and be in high spirits; I will sing praise to Your name, O Most High!

PSALM 9:2

THE PRAYER OF REJOICING

Twice in the passage from Philippians the apostle Paul tells us to rejoice. He urges us not to fret or have any anxiety about anything but to pray and give thanks to God *in* everything—not *after* everything is over.

If we wait until everything is perfect before rejoicing and giving thanks, we won't have much fun. Learning to enjoy life even in the midst of trying circumstances is one way we develop spiritual maturity. Paul also writes that we "are constantly being transfigured into His very own image in ever increasing splendor and from one degree of glory to another" (2 Corinthians 3:18). We need to learn how to enjoy the glory we are experiencing at each level of our development. Let's learn to pray a prayer of rejoicing and be glad in the Lord this day and every day along the way toward our goal.

When I first started my ministry, I depended on my circumstances for happiness. Finally the Lord showed me the doorway to happiness. He gave me a breakthrough by teaching me that fullness of joy is found in His *presence*—not in His *presents*! (Psalm 16:11.)

True joy comes from seeking God's face.

WHY PRAYER ISN'T ANSWERED

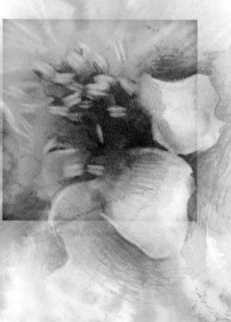

There's no power shortage in heaven,
but there is often a shortage
of prayers on earth.

GOD'S WORD FOR YOU

And, beloved, if our consciences (our hearts) do not accuse us [if they do not make us feel guilty and condemn us], we have confidence (complete assurance and boldness) before God,

And we receive from Him whatever we ask, because we [watchfully] obey His orders [observe His suggestions and injunctions, follow His plan for us] and [habitually] practice what is pleasing to Him.

1 JOHN 3:21-22

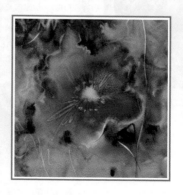

four

WHY PRAYER ISN'T ANSWERED

f there's anything I want to know for sure, it's that my prayers are going to be answered when I go to prayer. For a long time I was frustrated that I didn't see my prayers answered the way I would have liked. I knew that I had a loving heavenly Father Who delights in answering our petitions. But something wasn't working, so I sought the Lord. He began to instruct me in His Word about a number of obstacles that will hinder our prayer life. As I began to line up my life with the issues He showed me, I began to see more faith and power in my prayer life. And more answers to my prayers!

When you go to pray, do you feel uncomfortable? Maybe you're under condemnation, maybe you're not praying as a righteous person, or maybe you're regarding iniquity in your heart.

If we are going to get our prayers answered, then we are going to have to learn how to tap into the spiritual realm and allow the Holy Spirit to show us what obstacles He wants to remove from our lives. Then we must be obedient to what He shows us so that our prayers become fervent and effective for the Kingdom of God.

Allow the Holy Spirit to convict, cleanse, and fill you so that your prayers are filled with faith and power.

GOD'S WORD FOR YOU

And when that time comes, you will ask nothing of Me [you will need to ask Me no questions]. I assure you, most solemnly I tell you, that My Father will grant you whatever you ask in My Name [as presenting all that I AM]. [Exod. 3:14.]

Up to this time you have not asked a [single] thing in My Name [as presenting all that I AM]; but now ask and keep on asking and you will receive, so that your joy (gladness, delight) may be full and complete.

JOHN 16:23-24

PEOPLE DON'T PRAY BOLDLY

Our prayers aren't answered because we don't pray boldly. We need to pray more specifically and have the boldness to come before God and really ask Him for what we want and not be ashamed to make our requests known.

One of the major things that keeps people from praying boldly is they look at what they have done wrong instead of what Jesus has done right. The Bible teaches us plainly that God ". . . made Christ [virtually] to be sin Who knew no sin, so that in and through Him we might become [endued with, viewed as being in, and examples of] the righteousness of God" (2 Corinthians 5:21). Because we are righteous in Him, we can approach the throne of grace boldly with our needs (Hebrews 4:16).

John 16:23-24 tells us we can come boldly before the throne in Jesus' name. The name of Jesus is powerful. When I use Jesus' name in my prayers, it's not like some magic charm that I tack on to the end of everything. When I go in the name of Jesus, I'm saying, "Father, I come to you presenting today all that Jesus is—not what I am."

Don't be vague—be bold! You'll be surprised at the answers you'll get.

❧

God loves to answer our bold prayers
made in the name of Jesus.

GOD'S WORD FOR YOU

If I regard iniquity in my heart, the Lord will not hear me. [Prov. 15:29; 28:9; Isa. 1:15; John 9:31; James 4:3.]

PSALM 66:18

We know that God does not listen to sinners; but if anyone is God-fearing and a worshiper of Him and does His will, He listens to him.

JOHN 9:31

Iniquity in My Heart

Our prayers often do not get answered because we regard iniquity in our heart. David said, "If I regard iniquity in my heart, the Lord will not hear me" (Psalm 66:18). What that means, to put it bluntly, is that the Lord doesn't hear us when we pray if we come before Him with unclean hearts.

If there is sin your life, you will not be able to pray boldly or with confidence. When you're praying and you sense that you're not comfortable, stop and ask God why. Ask Him to reveal anything that's hidden. If He convicts you of something, don't be vague about it. Call it what it is—sin. We get release when we admit and confess our sin and bring it out in the open. He wants you to confess it so He can cleanse you and restore a clean conscience so that you can pray (1 John 1:9). There is power in truth and honesty when we come clean before the Lord and walk in the light.

Make sure your heart is clean before Him so your prayers are alive and energized by the Holy Spirit's power.

*God hears your prayers
when you approach Him with a clean heart.*

GOD'S WORD FOR YOU

For this reason we also, from the day we heard of it, have not ceased to pray and make [special] request for you, [asking] that you may be filled with the full (deep and clear) knowledge of His will in all spiritual wisdom [in comprehensive insight into the ways and purposes of God] and in understanding and discernment of spiritual things. . . .

COLOSSIANS 1:9

PEOPLE DON'T PRAY IN THE WILL OF GOD

Another reason why prayer is not answered is that people don't pray in the will of God. I'd like to say we're all led by the Spirit, and we all hear the voice of God. That's the place we're working toward, but we're not all there yet.

Sometimes it's not all that easy to decipher if what you're wanting is really God's will or just your flesh wanting it. In order to know God's will, you must know God's Word. Psalm 119:105 says, "Your word is a lamp to my feet and a light to my path." We must become students of the Word. Another issue comes into play regarding God's will: God's timing. To be out of God's timing is also to be out of His will. If I try to make it happen right now, then it's out of the will of God for today for my life.

First John 5:14 says, "and this is the confidence (the assurance, the privilege of boldness)." If I'm not praying in the will of God, He is not going to hook up with me and give me the power to pray with that boldness. But if you know the will of God concerning your prayer request, then faith will come out of your spirit to help you pray.

It's amazing what faith can do
when we know the will of God.

GOD'S WORD FOR YOU

. . . You do not have, because you do not ask. [I John 5:15.]

[Or] you do ask [God for them] and yet fail to receive, because you ask with wrong purpose and evil, selfish motives.

JAMES 4:2-3

Wrong Purpose and Motives

According to James 3:3, many prayers are not answered because people pray amiss. To pray amiss means we are praying with the "wrong purpose and evil, selfish motives." You could be praying for something that is the will of God, but you're praying for the wrong reason. When you first start to learn to pray, you're carnal, so you are going to pray carnally. You're going to pray many prayers for the wrong reason. We're not talking about what we do but why we're doing it.

Years ago I spent many hours praying for my ministry to grow. I wanted to look good in front of everybody, and I wanted to look successful. I wanted it to appear that I was obviously hearing from God. And I wanted those people to come to my meetings because the more people came, the better I looked.

Now I know who I am in Christ, and I know that my worth is not in my ministry. Back then I was praying with the wrong motive. Do you want your prayer life to be powerful and effective? Then before you go to prayer start checking your motives. Make sure you are praying for godly reasons with all humility.

When God finds humility and right motives,
His grace empowers our prayers.

GOD'S WORD FOR YOU

Truly I tell you, whoever says to this mountain, Be lifted up and thrown into the sea! and does not doubt at all in his heart but believes that what he says will take place, it will be done for him.

MARK 11:23

If any of you is deficient in wisdom, let him ask of the giving God [Who gives] to everyone liberally and ungrudgingly, without reproaching or faultfinding, and it will be given him.

Only it must be in faith that he asks with no wavering (no hesitating, no doubting). For the one who wavers (hesitates, doubts) is like the billowing surge out at sea that is blown hither and thither and tossed by the wind.

JAMES 1:5-6

216

Doubt and Unbelief

Another reason why prayer is not answered is that people have doubt and unbelief in their hearts. Doubt brings in confusion and often depression. It kills our faith and causes us to make negative confessions.

In Luke 18, Jesus told His disciples a parable to the effect that they ought always to pray and not to turn coward, faint, lose heart, and give up. He spoke of the widow who continued to plead her case before the unjust judge until he acted on her behalf. Jesus is saying that if an unjust judge can be moved by persistence, how much more will our loving heavenly Father be moved if we won't quit and give up because of doubt and unbelief.

We need to learn to move in the realm of the Spirit through faith, instead of relying on what we see in the natural. "For we walk by faith . . . not by sight or appearance" (2 Corinthians 5:7). Learn to stay in contact with God, always walking in His presence. If you begin to listen to the devil's lies, then soon doubt and unbelief come roaring back. Those fiery darts begin to wage war with your mind. Remember that doubt and unbelief are a product of the mind and our wrong focus.

Looking unto Jesus, the Author and Finisher of our faith, will stop doubt and unbelief.

GOD'S WORD FOR YOU

Enter into His gates with thanksgiving and a thank offering and into His courts with praise! Be thankful and say so to Him, bless and affectionately praise His name!

PSALM 100:4

I will give You thanks in the great assembly; I will praise You among a mighty throng.

PSALM 35:18

UNGRATITUDE

Prayer is often not answered because people are ungrateful. There are people who are grumblers, murmurers, faultfinders, and complainers. We have to be very careful that we're not like that. We need to be the kind of people who are thankful for what God is doing. If we are complaining and ungrateful all the time, we are going to have a hard time getting answers to our prayers.

If you want to see God work in your spouse, your children, your finances, your circumstances, or your job, you have to be grateful for what you already have.

God told me once, "Joyce, when people are praying and asking Me for things, if they don't have a thankful heart, that's a clear indication to Me that they're already grumbling trying to handle what they have." The devil's whole plan is to keep you dissatisfied with something all the time, grumbling, faultfinding, and complaining. When you are ungrateful, it holds you back from progressing and maturing in the Spirit.

God wants us to grow in maturity and become more like His Son Jesus. God's answer to ingratitude is a life filled with praise and thanksgiving.

Look for something today to be thankful for and offer up a prayer of praise and thanksgiving.

GOD'S WORD FOR YOU

So shall My word be that goes forth out of My mouth; it shall not return to Me void [without producing any effect, useless], but it shall accomplish that which I please and purpose, and it shall prosper in the thing for which I sent it.

ISAIAH 55:11

For the Word that God speaks is alive and full of power [making it active, operative, energizing, and effective]; it is sharper than any two-edged sword, penetrating to the dividing line of the breath of life (soul) and [the immortal] spirit, and of joints and marrow [of the deepest parts of our nature], exposing and sifting and analyzing and judging the very thoughts and purposes of the heart.

HEBREWS 4:12

PRAYERS NOT BASED ON THE WORD

We also fail to get answers to our prayers because they are not based on the Word of God. The prophet Isaiah says, "My word . . . shall not return to Me void." God says that His Word will always accomplish the purpose for which He has sent it. Learn the Word, speak the Word, pray the Word. Let God know that you are standing on the foundation of the Word.

When the devil tries to lie to you, quote him the Scriptures. The Bible says that the Word is "sharper than any two-edged sword" (Hebrews 4:12). We need to make sure that our prayers are prayers being produced by the Spirit of God and not our soulish prayers. If we stay in the Word, God will teach us when we're operating in the soul and when we're operating in the Spirit. The Holy Spirit uses the Word to judge the very thoughts and purposes of our hearts.

If I'm speaking God's Word in line with His will, then I can be assured that what I'm praying for will not come back empty-handed. God promises to fulfill His Word.

The Holy Spirit will quicken the Word to you to empower your prayers with faith and assurance.

GOD'S WORD FOR YOU

Death and life are in the power of the tongue, and they who indulge in it shall eat the fruit of it [for death or life]. [Matt. 12:37.]

PROVERBS 18:21

He who guards his mouth keeps his life, but he who opens wide his lips comes to ruin.

PROVERBS 13:3

NEGATIVE CONFESSION

If we want our prayers to be answered, we can't pray and then negate them with a negative confession. Let's say a mother is praying for a son who's having trouble in school. So she prays the prayer of faith and believes God for a breakthrough. Then she goes to lunch with two neighbors and spends the next hour saying, "I am so sick of these problems I'm having with this kid. Why me?"

This kind of negative confession wipes your prayer slate clean. You might as well not even waste your time praying until you make a decision to get your mouth in line with your prayers.

When the neighbors ask how your son is doing, say, "You know what? In the natural things have not changed a whole lot, but I'm praying for him, and I have assurance in my heart that God is doing a mighty work in his life."

Once you have laid hold of the answer through faith, then you need to make sure your confession is in agreement with what you've asked God to do. Don't let the devil trip you up when people ask you questions that you could answer negatively. Answer them with a positive confession of the Word of God.

*When you line up your mouth
with the positive confession of the Word of God,
you'll see amazing results.*

GOD'S WORD FOR YOU

And the servant of the Lord must not strive.

2 TIMOTHY 2:24 KJV

Let all bitterness and indignation and wrath (passion, rage, bad temper) and resentment (anger, animosity) and quarreling (brawling, clamor, contention) and slander (evil-speaking, abusive or blasphemous language) be banished from you, with all malice (spite, ill will, or baseness of any kind).

EPHESIANS 4:31

STRIFE

Strife is a thief and a robber that we must learn to recognize and deal with quickly. We must control strife before it controls us.

Strife is defined as "the act or state of fighting or quarreling, especially bitterly . . . discord." It is bickering, arguing, being involved in a heated disagreement, or shows up as an angry undercurrent. Strife is dangerous. It is a demonic force sent by Satan for the purpose of destruction.

Almost any time someone hurts us, or offends us, anger rises up within us. It is not sin to feel anger. But we must not act out the angry feelings in an ungodly way. We must not hold a grudge or get into bitterness, resentment, or unforgiveness.

A judgmental attitude is an open door for strife. We must remember that mercy triumphs over judgment (James 2:13 NIV). Judgment usually leads to gossip. Gossip begins to spread the strife from person to person. It gets us out of agreement, harmony, and unity. It actually moves us out of God's blessings.

When the temptation comes to judge others, and then spread our opinion through gossip and backbiting, we should remember this helpful hint: Let the one among us who is without sin cast the first stone (John 8:7).

Remember: God changes things through prayer and faith, not through judgment and gossip.

GOD'S WORD FOR YOU

And whenever you stand praying, if you have anything against anyone, forgive him and let it drop (leave it, let it go), in order that your Father Who is in heaven may also forgive you your [own] failings and shortcomings and let them drop.

But if you do not forgive, neither will your Father in heaven forgive your failings and shortcomings.

MARK 11:25-26

Then Peter came up to Him and said, Lord, how many times may my brother sin against me and I forgive him and let it go? [As many as] up to seven times?

Jesus answered him, I tell you, not up to seven times, but seventy times seven! [Gen. 4:24.]

MATTHEW 18:21-22

*U*NFORGIVENESS

One of the greatest reasons why prayer isn't answered among Christians is *unforgiveness*. In Mark 11 Jesus gave His disciples a command to forgive. And then He told them plainly that if they did not forgive, neither would their Father in heaven forgive them their failings and shortcomings. He was blunt with them because He knew what a stumbling block unforgiveness would be for their spiritual life.

It is important to note that forgiveness and having faith to move mountains comes in the same context. There is no power in speaking to a mountain if the heart is full of unforgiveness. Yet this problem is rampant among God's children. If there is anything that will short-circuit God from answering our prayers, it's a heart full of unforgiveness and bitterness toward others. You can't go into your prayer closet and expect God to move mountains for you or on behalf of others when you've hardened your heart with unforgiveness.

Jesus told Peter that he must be willing to forgive seven times seventy: 490 times. Jesus wanted to show His disciples that forgiveness was one of the main keys for unlocking the Kingdom of God in their lives if they wanted to have power in their prayers.

Extend abundant mercy and forgiveness
just as God forgave you in Christ.

PRAYER IN JESUS' NAME

We have been given the most powerful
Name in heaven and earth
to use when we pray. Let's use it!

GOD'S WORD FOR YOU

And [so that you can know and understand] what is the immeasurable and unlimited and surpassing greatness of His power in and for us who believe, as demonstrated in the working of His mighty strength,

Which He exerted in Christ when He raised Him from the dead and seated Him at His [own] right hand in the heavenly [places],

Far above all rule and authority and power and dominion and every name that is named [above every title that can be conferred], not only in this age and in this world, but also in the age and the world which are to come.

And He has put all things under His feet and has appointed Him the universal and supreme Head of the church [a headship exercised throughout the church], [Ps. 8:6.]

Which is His body, the fullness of Him Who fills all in all [for in that body lives the full measure of Him Who makes everything complete, and Who fills everything everywhere with Himself].

EPHESIANS 1:19-23

five
PRAYER IN JESUS' NAME

used the name of Jesus for many years without the results I had been told I could have. I began asking God why I was using the name that was supposed to have power over circumstances that were outside His will, and yet I was not seeing results. The Holy Spirit began to reveal to me that releasing the power in the name of Jesus requires faith in that name, that name that is so powerful that when it is mentioned in faith, every knee must bow in three realms—in heaven, on earth, and under the earth!

Jesus came from the highest heaven; He has been to the earth, and He has descended to Hades, under the earth, and now is seated again at the right hand of the Father in the highest heaven. He has made a full circle; therefore, He has filled everything and everywhere with Himself. He is seated above everything else and has a name above every other name. His name is the highest name, the most powerful name—and His name has been given to us to use in prayer!

*What an awesome privilege we have to use the name
of Jesus that is above every other name!*

GOD'S WORD FOR YOU

A woman, when she gives birth to a child, has grief (anguish, agony) because her time has come. But when she has delivered the child, she no longer remembers her pain (trouble, anguish) because she is so glad that a man (a child, a human being) has been born into the world.

So for the present you are also in sorrow (in distress and depressed); but I will see you again and [then] your hearts will rejoice, and no one can take from you your joy (gladness, delight).

And when that time comes, you will ask nothing of Me [you will need to ask Me no questions]. I assure you, most solemnly I tell you, that My Father will grant you whatever you ask in My Name [as presenting all that I AM]. [Exod. 3:14.]

Up to this time you have not asked a [single] thing in My Name [as presenting all that I AM]; but now ask and keep on asking and you will receive, so that your joy (gladness, delight) may be full and complete.

JOHN 16:21-24

His Name Takes His Place

Oh, how wonderful it would have been to have physically walked with Jesus. But He told His followers they would be better off when He went away, because then He would send His Spirit to dwell in every believer (John 16:7).

He told them that even though they were sorrowful at the news of His upcoming departure, they would rejoice again just as a woman has sorrow during her labor but rejoices when the child is born.

He said they would change their minds when they saw the glory of His Spirit in them and the power available to each of them through the privilege of using His name in prayer. He was literally giving to them—and has given to all those who believe in Him—His "power of attorney," the legal right to use His name. His name takes His place; His name represents Him.

Jesus has already been perfect for us. He has already pleased the Father for us; therefore, there is no pressure on us to feel that we must have a perfect record of right behavior before we can pray. Then when we come before the Father in Jesus' name, we can confess our sin, receive His forgiveness, and boldly make our requests known to Him.

When the name of Jesus is spoken by a believer in faith, all of heaven comes to attention.

GOD'S WORD FOR YOU

If ye shall ask any thing in my name, I will do it.

JOHN 14:14 KJV

Then some of the traveling Jewish exorcists (men who adjure evil spirits) also undertook to call the name of the Lord Jesus over those who had evil spirits, saying, I solemnly implore and charge you by the Jesus Whom Paul preaches!

Seven sons of a certain Jewish chief named Sceva were doing this.

But [one] evil spirit retorted, Jesus I know, and Paul I know about, but who are you?

Then the man in whom the evil spirit dwelt leaped upon them, mastering two of them, and was so violent against them that they dashed out of that house [in fear], stripped naked and wounded.

ACTS 19:13-16

JESUS' NAME IS NOT MAGIC

The name of Jesus is not a "magic word" or a ritualistic incantation to be added to the end of a prayer to insure its effectiveness.

In the Book of Acts we read of the mighty miracles that God did through the life of Paul. God honored Paul's faith when he spoke the name of Jesus. Certain Jewish exorcists, however, attempted to use the name of Jesus as if it were a simple incantation to be said. The Bible says the "man in whom the evil spirit dwelt leaped upon them, mastering two of them" (Acts 19:16). The spirit spoke and said it knew Jesus and Paul but not them.

If we are going to pray and use the powerful name of Jesus, then we must be in a living, obedient relationship with Him. Then the power of the Holy Spirit will flow out of our lives and deliver us and others from the devil's bondages.

All Spirit-led prayer involves praying the will of God, not the will of man! It is impossible to pray the will of God without knowing the Word of God. Yes, God certainly pays attention to the prayers that come to Him in Jesus' name, but not ones that are outside of His will.

You must know Jesus as Lord
before you can use His name in power.

GOD'S WORD FOR YOU

Behold! I have given you authority and power to trample upon serpents and scorpions, and [physical and mental strength and ability] over all the power that the enemy [possesses]; and nothing shall in any way harm you.

LUKE 10:19

And His name, through and by faith in His name, has made this man whom you see and recognize well and strong.

ACTS 3:16

THE NAME OF JESUS IS POWER

The name of Jesus is power. No loving parent would release power to a baby, because the parent knows the child would get hurt. Parents don't withhold power from their children to hurt them, but to help them or to keep them safe. Our heavenly Father is the same way. He tells us what is available to us, and then by His Spirit helps us mature to the point where we can handle what He desires to give us.

I believe the power in the name of Jesus is unlimited. I also believe that our heavenly Father releases it to us as He knows we can handle it properly.

When Jesus began to talk to His disciples about the privilege of praying in His name and having their requests granted, He said, "I *solemnly* tell you . . ." I believe that the power of God is a solemn responsibility. God's power is not a toy! It is not to be released to people who are only playing, but to those who are seriously ready to get on with God's program for their lives.

As you continue to grow and mature in Christ,
you can look for exciting new dimensions
in your walk with the Lord.

GOD'S WORD FOR YOU

And it shall be that whoever shall call upon the name of the Lord [invoking, adoring, and worshiping the Lord— Christ] shall be saved.

ACTS 2:21

In Times of Crisis

Years ago before seatbelt laws, a friend of mine was driving with his young son through a busy intersection one day. The car door on the passenger side was not secured tightly, and he made a sharp turn. The car door flew open, and the little boy rolled out right into traffic! The last thing my friend saw was a set of car wheels just about on top of his son. All he knew to do was cry, "Jesus!"

He stopped his car and ran to his son. To his amazement, his son was perfectly all right. But the man driving the car that had almost hit the child was hysterical.

"Man, don't be upset!" my friend said. "My son is okay. Just thank God you were able to stop!"

"You don't understand!" the man responded. "I never touched my brakes!"

Although there was nothing man could do, the name of Jesus prevailed, and the boy's life was spared.

In times of crisis, call upon the name of Jesus. The more you and I see how faithful He is in times of need and crises, the more we witness the power in His name over situations and circumstances, the more our faith is developed in His name.

There is power in the name of Jesus
for every crisis we will ever face.

GOD'S WORD FOR YOU

Let this same attitude and purpose and [humble] mind be in you which was in Christ Jesus: [Let Him be your example in humility:]

Who, although being essentially one with God and in the form of God [possessing the fullness of the attributes which make God God], did not think this equality with God was a thing to be eagerly grasped or retained,

But stripped Himself [of all privileges and rightful dignity], so as to assume the guise of a servant (slave), in that He became like men and was born a human being,

And after He had appeared in human form, He abased and humbled Himself [still further] and carried His obedience to the extreme of death, even the death of the cross!

Therefore [because He stooped so low] God has highly exalted Him and has freely bestowed on Him the name that is above every name.

PHILIPPIANS 2:5-8

OBEDIENCE AND THE NAME OF JESUS

Jesus became extremely obedient; therefore, He was given a name that is above every other name. But let's not get so caught up in the power these verses set forth that we forget the obedience they describe.

John 14:15 says: "If you [really] love Me, you will keep (obey) My commands."

Obedience is important!

Now I realize that the ability is not in us (apart from the Lord's help) to be perfectly obedient, but if we have a willing heart within us, and if we do what we can do, then He will send His Spirit to do what we cannot do.

I am not suggesting that the power in Jesus' name won't work without perfect obedience. I am making a point that the power in the name of Jesus will not be released to anyone who is not seriously pressing toward the mark of the high calling in Christ (Philippians 3:14 KJV), which is maturity—and maturity requires extreme obedience. Extreme obedience requires a willingness to suffer in the flesh, in a godly way, for example, by denying yourself something you want that you know isn't good for you, if need be, in order to know and do the will of God.

In order for us to experience the freedom Jesus purchased for us, we need to be obedient to His Word.

GOD'S WORD FOR YOU

For [instance] a married woman is bound by law to her husband as long as he lives; but if her husband dies, she is loosed and discharged from the law concerning her husband.

Likewise, my brethren, you have undergone death as to the Law through the [crucified] body of Christ, so that now you may belong to Another, to Him Who was raised from the dead in order that we may bear fruit for God.

ROMANS 7:2, 4

But the person who is united to the Lord becomes one spirit with Him.

1 CORINTHIANS 6:17

To Use the Name, You Must Be "Married"!

I was studying about the name of Jesus when the Lord spoke to my heart. He said, "Joyce, when you married Dave, you got his name and the power of all the name Meyer means." He reminded me that I can use the name Dave Meyer and get the same results that Dave could get himself if he were with me. I can even go to the bank and get Dave Meyer's money, because when two people get married, all the property of each now belongs to the other.

Through this example of everyday life, the Holy Spirit was attempting to teach me that although I had a relationship with the Lord, it was more like a courtship than a marriage. I liked "to go on dates" with Him, but when "the date" was over, I wanted to go my own way. I wanted all of Him and His favor and benefits, but I did not want to give Him all of myself.

The apostle Paul tells us that we have died to the law of sin and death and are now married to Another so that we can bear fruit for Him. Remember, you cannot legally use the name until after the marriage to Jesus.

Jesus is the Bridegroom, and we are His Bride.
That is how God the Father has planned it,
and that is the only way His plan will work properly.

GOD'S WORD FOR YOU

Then Jesus called together the Twelve [apostles] and gave them power and authority over all demons, and to cure diseases,

And He sent them out to announce and preach the kingdom of God and to bring healing.

LUKE 9:1-2

EXERCISING AUTHORITY IN THE NAME

As believers we need to recognize that the power of attorney gives the right to *command* in Jesus' name.

We pray and ask the Father for things in Jesus' name, but we command the enemy in that name. We speak to circumstances and principalities and powers, using the authority that has been given us by virtue of the power of attorney invested in us by Jesus Himself. In exercising our deliverance ministry, we don't lay hands on a person and begin to pray for God to cast it out. We command it to come out in the name of Jesus.

Before we can exercise this authority, we have already prayed to the Father in Jesus' name. Now we go and use the power He has granted us, and we exercise the authority inherent in the name of His Son Jesus.

The same thing applies to healing the sick. There are times to pray the prayer of faith in the name of Jesus (James 5:15); there are times to anoint with oil (James 5:14); but there are also times simply to command or speak in the name of Jesus.

Spend time daily with the Lord. Fellowship, ask, pray, seek, and come out of that time equipped for the job at hand.

When you go to do the work of the Kingdom, exercise your authority in Jesus' name.

GOD'S WORD FOR YOU

But Peter said, Silver and gold (money) I do not have; but what I do have, that I give to you: in [the use of] the name of Jesus Christ of Nazareth, walk!

ACTS 3:6

Do Not Be Selfish With the Name

I believe there are those who have heard messages about the power that is available to them in the name of Jesus, and who are busy using that name hoping to get everything they have ever wanted. We certainly can and should use the name in our own behalf, as long as we use it to fulfill God's will for our life and not our own. However, there is another aspect of using the name in prayer: *using the name of Jesus to pray for others*.

That is really what the apostles were doing in the book of Acts. Jesus had sent them out empowered with His authority and His name, and they got busy trying to help others with it. They were using the name of Jesus to bring salvation, healing, deliverance, and the baptism of the Holy Spirit to all those for whom Jesus had died who did not yet know Him.

Take the name of Jesus and love people with it. When you see a need, whisper a prayer in Jesus' name. God has entrusted every believer with two ministries: the ministry of *reconciliation* and the ministry of *intercession*.

So much can be accomplished in the earth as believers begin to use the name of Jesus unselfishly.

GOD'S WORD FOR YOU

Now to Him Who, by (in consequence of) the [action of His] power that is at work within us, is able to [carry out His purpose and] do superabundantly, far over and above all that we [dare] ask or think [infinitely beyond our highest prayers, desires, thoughts, hopes, or dreams].

EPHESIANS 3:20

EXCEEDINGLY, ABUNDANTLY ABOVE AND BEYOND

When I pray about all the people who are hurting, I have a strong desire to help them all. I feel that my desire is bigger than my ability, and it is—but it is not bigger than God's ability!

When the thing we are facing in our life or ministry looms so big in our eyes that our mind goes "tilt," we need to *think in the spirit*. In the natural, many things are impossible. But God wants us to believe for great things, make big plans, and expect Him to do things so great it leaves us with our mouths hanging open in awe.

God does not usually call people who are capable; if He did, He would not get the glory. He frequently chooses those who, in the natural, feel as if they are in completely over their heads but who are ready to stand up on the inside and take bold steps of faith. They have learned the secret of using Jesus' name and depending on that "superabundant" power that works within them.

When our desires seem overwhelmingly big, and we don't see the way to accomplish them, we should remember that even though we don't know the way, we know the Waymaker!

Because of His abundant power within us, God has a way for us to do everything He places in our heart.

GOD'S WORD FOR YOU

And Moses said to God, Behold, when I come to the Israelites and say to them, The God of your fathers has sent me to you, and they say to me, What is His name? What shall I say to them?

And God said to Moses, I AM WHO I AM and WHAT I AM, and I WILL BE WHAT I WILL BE; and He said, You shall say this to the Israelites, I AM has sent me to you!

EXODUS 3:13-14

Jesus replied, I assure you, most solemnly I tell you, before Abraham was born, I AM.

JOHN 8:58

THE NAME OF GOD IS I AM

I have pondered these verses for a long time. To me, they are awesome scriptures that hold much more than we may realize. What was God saying to Moses when He referred to Himself as I AM?

God is saying He is so much, so great, that there is no way to describe Him properly. How can we describe in one name Someone Who is everything? God said to Moses, "I AM can take care of anything you encounter. Whatever you need, I AM it. Either I have it or I can get it. If it doesn't exist, I will create it. I have everything covered, not only now, but for all time. Relax!"

Jesus responded to His disciples the same way God the Father responded to Moses. Revelation 1:8 declares Jesus to be the Alpha and the Omega. That means the first and the last, the beginning and the end. He has always been and always will be.

Our finite human minds cannot expand far enough even to begin to comprehend the limitless power that has been invested in His glorious name.

When we pray in the name of Jesus, we are praying in the name of the great I AM—the omnipotent God of all eternity.

The Lord is the Ever-Present I AM. Always with us.
Everything we need, or ever will need.

JOYCE MEYER

JOYCE MEYER has been teaching the Word of God
since 1976 and in full-time ministry since 1980.
She is the bestselling author of more than sixty
inspirational books, including *In Pursuit of Peace*,
How to Hear from God, *Knowing God Intimately*, and
Battlefield of the Mind. She has also released thousands
of teaching cassettes and a complete video library.
Joyce's *Enjoying Everyday Life* radio and television
programs are broadcast around the world, and she
travels extensively conducting conferences. Joyce and
her husband, Dave, are the parents of four grown
children and make their home in St. Louis, Missouri.

Additional copies of this book are available from your local bookstore.

If this book has changed your life, we would like to hear from you.

Please write us at:

Joyce Meyer Ministries
P.O. Box 655 • Fenton, MO 63026

or call: (636) 349-0303

Internet Address: www.joycemeyer.org

In Canada, write: Joyce Meyer Ministries Canada, Inc.
Lambeth Box 1300 • London, ON N6P 1T5

or call: (636) 349-0303

In Australia, write: Joyce Meyer Ministries—Australia
Locked Bag 77 • Mansfield Delivery Centre
Queensland 4122

or call: (07) 3349 1200

In England, write: Joyce Meyer Ministries
P.O. Box 1549 • Windsor • SL4 1GT

or call: 01753 831102